Attracting Birds and Other Wildlife to Your Yard

Attracting Birds and Other Wildlife to Your Yard

by William J. Weber, D.V.M.

photographs by the author

Holt, Rinehart and Winston / New York

Library of Congress Cataloging in Publication Data

Weber, William J.
  Attracting birds and other wildlife to your yard.

  Includes bibliographies and index.
  Summary: Presents techniques of attracting birds and
animals to the average city or suburban lot.
  1. Birds, Attracting of—Juvenile literature.
2. Wildlife attracting—Juvenile literature. [1. Birds
—Attracting. 2. Wildlife attracting] I. Title.
QL676.5.W375   639.9'78   81-7049
ISBN 0-03-056224-4   AACR2

ISBN 0-03-056224-4

For Bill and John,
my sons and my friends.

Contents

Attracting Birds and Other Wildlife to Your Yard

Native bison were exterminated from United States land in 1887. The bison now found in the U.S.A. are descended from animals imported from Canada.

Introduction

Wildlife and wild creatures are part of our American heritage. In the early days of our history, there was an abundance of wildlife. Wildlife provided food, clothing, and shelter to the pioneers and provided the means for them to cross the continent. And yet we treated our wildlife shabbily.

Bison were hunted wastefully for hides and tongues until the last of millions disappeared in 1887. Deer, turkey, elk, and antelope went from abundance to a tiny few in the early 1900's. Pigeons, ducks, and geese were killed without care or regard to whether enough survived to carry on their species.

At last a stirring of the national conscience caused people to speak out. In 1904 President Teddy Roosevelt created fifty-one National Wildlife Refuges. Congress passed laws to protect migratory birds. As a result, many of the protected creatures were able to survive and their populations to rebound.

Can you imagine living in a world without wildlife—without birds? Think what it would be like never to see a deer slipping through wooded shadows, or a squirrel scurrying across the grass. Would it make a difference to you if there

1

were no birdsongs during the quiet of the day? If the loss of these things would bother you, you can help by offering your support to worthwhile conservation efforts or, better yet, by creating your own minisanctuary where wild creatures find a chance to rest and have a bite of food.

Some of the ways you can provide shelter and food to enhance the survival of wildlife will be covered in this book. The emphasis here is on attracting wildlife to the average city or suburban lot. It will be up to you to select the ideas that appeal to you and that fit your situation best.

I agree with Roger Tory Peterson, the author-ornithologist, who once told the Canadian Wildlife Federation, ''There is a disbelief in the importance of your contribution. . . . My urgent plea is that you snap out of it, that you claim kinship with the creatures outside your back door, for your sake as well as theirs.''

◄1►

Why Attract Birds and Wild Creatures to Your Yard?

Why would people want to go to the trouble of attracting birds and other wild creatures to their yards? I can't answer for everyone, but I can tell you some of the reasons that I have heard others express and the reasons I personally find it such a rewarding effort.

People often start feeding birds in an offhand manner, usually by passing out their mealtime crumbs. They find they like seeing birds, and soon they fix feeders and start buying birdseed to supplement the foods they have on hand. The more enjoyment they have in watching birds come to feed, the more they become involved in the feeding process.

It is not only a visual pleasure but a source of inner satisfaction to know they might be helping these exuberant feathered creatures make it through another year. For birds must endure daily hardships. They spend most of their waking hours searching for food to live, and life is short for most of them. In addition, they must face rain, cold, predators, and the hazards of migration. How great to be able to offer them a few moments in a quiet sanctuary where they can rest and eat.

Any sanctuary you create that appeals to wildlife will also be a restful, peaceful sanctuary for you. And which of us hasn't felt the need to retreat to a quiet place where we can get away from everything for a while and revive our spirits.

There are also practical considerations. The trees, shrubs, and flowers that you plant for wild creatures increase the value of your own property.

In addition, each songbird we help repays us double. It gets rid of a tremendous number of harmful insects that annoy us, destroy our plants, eat crops, and spread disease.

Ralph Opp, an Oregon wildlife biologist, states, "One songbird eats insects equivalent to 20 percent of its body weight daily. A warbler may eat as many as 3,500 aphids in one hour. A swallow may catch over 2,000 flying insects in a day." Another biologist says that the chickadees in Michigan destroy eight billion insects each year.

Other studies show that in one year, birds in farming areas eat more than 300 weed seeds for each square foot of soil surface. The U.S. Department of Agriculture estimates that each songbird performs $10.00 worth of service a year in a yard or garden. Imagine, a single bobwhite quail eats 5,000 to 15,000 weed seeds in a single day.

Yes, birds serve us and all mankind.

If you are still not convinced that it is worthwhile to help wild creatures, consider these points. The toads we attract eat slugs, flies, mosquitos, and other flying insects. Owls eliminate mice and rats, pests in all areas of the country. Beneficial snakes also destroy mice, rats, and other rodents. Woodpeckers eat grubs and insects that damage trees. Flickers, another

A bobwhite quail will eat 5,000 to 15,000 weed seeds in a single day.

type of woodpecker, eat ants that do damage and also hurt when they bite. Skunks, opossums, and raccoons feed on harmful grubs and other insects along with the other things in their diet. Sparrow hawks feed on large grasshoppers that destroy plants and crops. They also eat small rodents that destroy crops.

An owl feeds on mice, rats, and other rodents, keeping their number under control.

We could go on, making a case to justify the wild world, but the most important reason to help them is because we want to and because we enjoy doing it. For if there weren't a single economic gain, the splash of bright color as the birds fly about, and the sound of their songs as they forage and nest close by, would be ample reward.

If seeing a cottontail hopping across your lawn at dusk doesn't make you smile, if hearing quail call doesn't make you pause and listen to their answering call, perhaps this book will change your mind.

But if you thrill to the sight of geese flying overhead or hummingbirds manuevering for nectar from a flower, or you find yourself watching for the first birds of spring, then you are probably a kindred spirit. In either case stay with me, and together let us find the fun and satisfaction in attracting wild creatures.

‹2›
Attracting Birds

Before considering what birds we can attract, let's discuss the various types of birds. We will not classify by physical characteristics, feathers, songs, and other criteria the ornithologist (one who studies birdlife) uses. Rather, we will group birds by similarities of eating habits, size, nesting places, and other things you can readily see for yourself. This is one way to determine what appeals to and attracts different birds.

Let us, first, look at the eating habits. The largest group of birds that you can attract to your yard are the seed-eating birds. Examples would be blue jays, cardinals, red-winged blackbirds, some woodpeckers, grosbeaks, redpolls, and sparrows. You can expect to attract these birds by putting up feeders and offering various types of seeds. Certain seed-eating birds will not land on the usual feeder, but will feed on the ground. I am speaking of the mourning dove, quail, and pheasant, among others.

Some songbirds that don't prefer seeds will be attracted to a feeder in which you have placed beef suet or fat. Red-headed woodpeckers, red-bellied woodpeckers, flickers, and sapsuckers appreciate suet.

You can attract still other birds by offering high-energy fat in the form of congealed bacon grease, meat drippings mixed with seeds, or fat in the form of peanut butter mixed with seeds. Birds that enjoy this mixture are red-bellied woodpeckers, chickadees, nuthatches, and a whole host of birds.

Another category would be insect- and fruit-eating birds, such as mockingbirds, scarlet tanagers, and orioles. They frequently can be attracted to the feeder with raisins, sections of orange, bits of dog food, bits of apple, and other exotic foods. If you put out half a grapefruit peel filled with bits of fruit, migrating warblers and thrushes will often respond.

If you want to attract the shy, gentle hummingbirds, you will use hummingbird feeders that contain the sweet nectar they enjoy. To attract the colorful yellow goldfinches, you will offer tiny black thistle seeds.

The point is that each time you add something different as a food, you will attract another group of birds. For example, if you place only cracked corn in your feeders, it will attract a few birds; but adding millet, milo, and other small grains adds the variety that other birds like, so you will have many more visitors.

We go into greater detail on how to make and set up a feeder in a later chapter. For now, realize that the first thing you must learn is what birds are in your area at specific times of the year, and what those birds like to eat. You can attract the birds you like by appealing to their appetites.

You need not supply all their food at a feeder. Birds also like the berries and fruits of certain trees and bushes. The hard red berries of the pyracantha, holly bushes, and red cedar attract cedar waxwings, bluebirds, sparrows, robins, purple finches, and cardinals. The soft fruit of the mulberry tree is a

To attract birds like the mockingbird you must plant fruit and berries, for these birds seldom visit feeders.

delight to robins, mockingbirds, and a great many other birds that enjoy its sweet fruit.

Food isn't the only way to attract birds. Shelter from weather, protection from predators, and a place to nest also convince birds to visit your yard. Birds are much more likely to use your feeders if there is a bush or shrub nearby that they can duck into if a hawk sails by. They will come to eat if you feed them. Certainly, they are more apt to stay if you offer them a good nesting spot.

Thrashers, field sparrows, song sparrows, catbirds, buntings, cardinals, cedar waxwings, and goldfinches prefer to nest in dense shrubbery close to the ground.

Orioles, robins, doves, some warblers, red-eyed vireos, scarlet tanagers, grosbeaks, peewees, redstarts, and blue jays prefer to build their nests in the limbs of the taller trees. You can select and plant mulberry, cherry, or nut trees to appeal to them.

Tall trees are favored by woodpeckers. They can enlarge a rotten spot and create a cavity for a nest home. Next year the woodpecker will hollow out a new home somewhere else. The hole it made this year will be used by chickadees, titmice, or even flying squirrels. Or else another woodpecker may find it and enlarge it for its home. The enlarged hole will later become the nest of a gray squirrel or a screech owl. All cavities are important in attracting wild creatures.

Since nest holes are so vital to so many wild creatures, you can help by creating a substitute. You can build houses that function as nesting cavities and place them in the trees to attract woodpeckers, owls, and squirrels.

We will discuss how to build houses for specific birds in greater detail later. For now, it is enough to realize how useful houses are in attracting certain birds and some small mammals to your yard.

Easy-to-build houses for wrens and bluebirds are the best way to attract these birds. Screech owls, chickadees, flickers, flycatchers, and many other birds will use houses if you will build them. Robins, doves, and a few other birds will some-

A male wood duck is an attractive, colorful ornament to any yard, but it must have a nest box near the water.

times nest on a simple shelf that has been placed in a tree. If there is water nearby, consider building a few wood duck houses, for homes are in short supply for them, too.

If you don't wish to be involved in building houses and nest cavities, you can attract many birds to your yard if you give them space to build their own homes.

Some birds nest on the ground. For these birds, you can leave a strip of your lawn unmowed. Let it grow back to native grasses and wild flowers. This will provide an attractive nesting spot for quail, ovenbirds, juncos, veeries, and towhees. A strip allowed to grow up along a lake, pond, river, or creek will attract birds, too. Green herons, bitterns, coots, red-winged blackbirds, yellow-headed blackbirds, and many types of wild ducks will find such spots lovely nesting sites if they aren't disturbed too frequently.

Water, in the simplest of containers or birdbaths, is appreciated by the birds that come into your yard. A birdbath, pond, stream, or lake will attract birds to drink, forage, rest, and nest nearby.

If you are going to be successful in attracting birds to your yard, it is most important to get to know the birds that are normal for your area. Most bird books include maps that show where the specific birds nest and live in the warm months, where they are found during migration, and where they stay in winter.

Read and gather information on the birds you like and are interested in. As you read on in this book, make notes of the things you can do, or provide, that will cause the bird or birds you like to choose your yard as their home. It may be a specific food or a certain nest requirement. When you know these points, you have the key to attracting them.

·3·
Choosing Plants
and Trees for Wildlife

The groups of plants for you to consider for your sanctuary are grasses and wild flowers, low shrubs, tall shrubs, vines, small trees, large trees, and evergreens. We shall consider particular advantages or benefits offered by each group to the wild creatures.

Grasses, weeds, and wild flowers offer a variety of good choices. Fortunately, there has been a change in style in many neighborhoods. It is no longer necessary to have your whole yard be a well-manicured lawn to be acceptable to your neighbors. Landscapers are encouraging patches of native wild flowers and grasses to grow. This has several advantages.

Most native flowers and grasses produce fruits or seeds that are important wildlife foods. In addition, most native plants do not require extra fertilizer or water, and most reseed themselves. Generally they do not require a great deal of care. Certainly they don't need the regular mowing or edging involved in caring for a manicured lawn.

Among wild grasses, choose those that have good crops of seeds to serve as wildlife food. Your local librarian can steer you to books that discuss the grasses native to your area. Many local garden clubs have projects to establish both native grasses and wild flowers. They can tell you not only the benefits of various plants, but also where to obtain seeds. Many of the vegetable seed catalogues now list the seeds of wild flowers from all areas of the country.

Take advantage of the services of your local county agent, an excellent source of information. This person will be listed in the telephone directory, under county offices, as County Extension Agent or County Agricultural Agent. These men or women are usually familiar with the native grasses and some of the native wild flowers. I have found most county agents to be interested and helpful in locating seeds for wildlife projects.

Before you plant any seeds, it is a good idea to have the soil in your yard tested for the essential nutrients needed to grow plants. The county extension agent can help here too, for most soil samples to be tested are submitted to this office. In most states there is no charge for soil analysis, but some offices may have a small fee.

In an average yard, a soil sample, to be of value, should be collected from several spots. Take soil from at least four spots that represent the typical soil in your yard. Dig shallow holes four to six inches deep. Take two tablespoonfuls of earth from this depth from each site, and place them all in a jar or coffee can. Be sure to collect an equal amount from each site. If you have a small yard, you can't have room to plant much and a sample from one spot will be enough. If you have a large yard, take samples from eight spots. If your yard has different types of terrain or soil, such as a steep hillside, or the edge of a pond or creek, take *separate* samples from each different place. If the terrain is relatively similar all over, do not separate the samples.

Secure the can, shake it, and mix the sample well. Submit it to the county agent's office in person or by mail. If you mail it, be sure to include a letter explaining how and where you collected your sample and request a soil analysis.

A report will be mailed to you indicating what minerals are deficient in your soil, the pH, or acidity, of your soil, and recommending the fertilizer or other additives required to bring the soil up to average growing standards.

Remember, however, that many wild flowers will grow only in poor, unfertilized soil. Fertilizer makes most grasses grow abundantly, but may not be good for wild flowers. Generally you can tell if this will be so, for the description of the flower on the seed packet frequently tells you what conditions the flower likes.

If this flower is normally found in dry, sandy, poor soil, don't fertilize the area. If it grows best along the borders of meadows where the meadow meets the woods, you will probably need some fertilizer, unless your soil is naturally rich or contains plenty of organic material. If the package says that the flower is normally found in deep shade, in heavily forested areas, be sure and plant among the shrubbery and in the shade of the trees. Normally these plants will need extra water and just a little fertilizer to get established.

The seeds of most grasses and wild flowers will grow if they are just scattered over the ground. If you live in a northern area, the best time to broadcast the seeds is during late winter, while the ground is frozen and there is a light soft snow on the ground. Planting at this time has several important advantages.

The seeds sink into the soft snow, where they are hidden and escape becoming bird food. As the snow begins to melt, the seeds are well moistened, which makes them sprout better.

Normally when soil freezes it heaves up in spots where moisture collects. This irregular surface makes little cavities that capture the seeds as the snow melts, so they don't float away. Then, as the soil thaws and settles, many of the seeds are covered naturally.

If you live in an area where you don't have snow and frozen ground, scatter your seeds, then scatter several pailfuls of fine topsoil over them, and water the planted area well every day for about three days. After that, water every third or fourth day for another five or six waterings. This way most of the seeds will germinate and get a good start before they have to make it on their own. During a real dry spell, water for a longer period at about weekly intervals, until the plants appear to be growing well.

Once the native plants get established, the stems catch and attract leaves and other materials blown about by the wind. These materials act as a soil covering, or mulch, to hold in soil moisture. As this material rots, it adds humus, a natural fertilizer, to the soil. Trapping leaves and other materials, the flower stems conserve moisture and replenish nutrients. They literally take care of themselves.

One of the best and most widely used plants for wildlife, and one that grows over most of the country, is called bicolor lespedeza. This plant has several advantages: It grows readily in poor soil. It is a legume, which means it has the ability to take nitrogen from the air and convert it to fertilizer in its roots. This fertilizer can be used by other plants. In other words, it works naturally to enrich the soil.

It is a clover-type plant that rabbits and other creatures eat and enjoy, and it has seeds that quail and other seed eaters find delicious. If it grows in your area, you may wish to plant some initially to improve your soil and to provide an immediate food source. Bicolor lespedeza is a perennial, which means that it grows every year from its original seed, so you only have to plant it once.

Among the grasses you may consider Indian grass, little bluestem, timothy, fescue, bluegrass, orchard grass, and many others. Find out which two or three do best where you live and plant a mixture of these.

Among the wild flowers there are many to choose from: day lilies, horsemint, daisies, butterfly weed, bergamot, and black-eyed Susans. We could write a whole book on just wild flowers for different areas. Choose those that you like, that grow well in your area and soil, and that offer some food to wild creatures.

While your native plants are getting established, plant a few sunflowers. These will provide seeds for your feeder, or you can just let the birds harvest them themselves. Sunflowers are generally easy to grow. They are planted in rows or clumps, one to two inches deep in the soil. They produce a nutritious food to tide the wild creatures over while your native food plants get established.

One more important point: If you want this unmowed strip or area to remain a grass-wild flower area, you must be sure it is cut back once a year. In the normal progression, shrubs move into open fields, then the small trees, then larger trees—always working toward what is called a climax forest. If you want this desirable area of grass and wild flowers to remain, you have to prevent the woody shrubs and trees from moving in and taking over.

You do this by taking an example from nature. In nature, wildfires kill the woody plants periodically. You can burn your strip during late winter or very early spring. But you must first take some preliminary steps, then you must be careful: 1. Make sure that there are no local ordinances that forbid doing so. 2. Get the consent of your neighbors. 3. Notify the local police or forest service. 4. Have enough help on hand to make sure your fire stays confined to your own yard.

Burn when it is not windy, and when the dead grasses are not completely dry, so they burn more slowly. A few members of your family and a couple of neighbor friends armed with brooms, shovels, and garden hoses should have no difficulty keeping the fire where it belongs until it burns itself out. Common sense and sufficient help keep this from being a dangerous or reckless procedure. After the fire, the wild flowers will sprout from the seeds shed earlier.

As an alternative, you can mow the grass-wild flower area. This should be done in the fall after all flowers and grasses have gone to seed, or, if you live in a cold area, after frost has killed back most of the plants. Because not all of the plants are dead, the grass-wild flower area ideally should not be cut closer than about six inches above the ground level. It is difficult to get most mowers to cut that high, but a hand sickle, if you know how to wield one, works well at this height. You cannot cover a large area with a sickle, and you may have to use your lawn mower set as high as it will go.

There are several attractive vines beneficial to wildlife. Greenbrier has dark berries on it that are a rich food source for chipmunks, grouse, thrushes, and other wildlife. Honeysuckle has attractive, scented blossoms that furnish nectar, and the dense growth of vines makes good cover and nesting sites for birds and wild creatures. Honeysuckle berries are favored by purple finches, pine grosbeaks, and others. Trumpet honeysuckle, a red flower, attracts hummingbirds and furnishes nectar to a host of insects that serve as food for birds. Wild grapes, too, have fruit that can be a food source to wild creatures.

Among the plants that are neither vines nor shrubs, but in between, is the multiflora rose. It is always recommended as a

A chipmunk harvests rose hips, eating some and storing seeds in its underground storeroom.

plant beneficial to wildlife. It has beautiful flowers in spring and summer. In the fall and winter the seedy fruit, called rose hip, is an important food for bluebirds, robins, cedar wax-wings, white-throated sparrows, juncos, catbirds, quail, and pheasants. This thorny bush grows rank and heavy. With all its thorns it offers good nesting sites for birds and good cover for small mammals and other wild creatures. The thorns will not hurt them. But it does have a serious disadvantage.

The seeds are easily spread by birds, and this plant has become a serious pest in many farming areas. So serious are its inroads that state funds are being spent on control programs to eradicate it. So before you begin planting the multiflora rose as a hedge and food plant, consider whether your neighbors will want it invading their yards or farms. If there is any doubt, plant something else.

The more familiar common blackberry is classed as a low shrub. It seems to spring up wherever ground is left undisturbed. You seldom need to plant it unless you are well into the city. As long as there are blackberry plants anywhere in the vicinity, volunteers will spring up on your planting from seeds carried by birds.

The elderberry is another summer fruiting bush that makes an excellent wildlife food. It favors damp moist areas, and likes plenty of sunshine. It grows well and needs little care. You plant it from roots during its dormant season (in fall, trees and shrubs lose their leaves and stop growing; this resting period is called the dormant time, and is the best time for transplanting bare-root shrubs and trees—see p. 123).

Highbush cranberry, red cedar, bush honeysuckle, serviceberry, pyracantha, sumac, red osier dogwood, and hawthorne are just a few of the choices among the shrubs that produce berries and nesting habitats.

Probably two of the very best wildlife shrubs are the Russian olive and the autumn olive. Neither is a native of this country, but both are widespread now. Russian olive grows all through the west from the Pacific Ocean to the Mississippi River, from sea level to 8,000 feet. The autumn olive grows well in the east from Maine to northern Georgia, and westward to Missouri.

Several things make these shrubby trees attractive as wild-life plants. They have great clusters of berries. The Russian olive has white berries, the autumn olive reddish-brown ones. Both ripen in the fall, and the ripe berries stay on the bushy shrubs through the winter or until they all have been eaten. As many as 42 kinds of birds and many mammals are known to enjoy feeding on these berries. In addition, the tall bushes grow dense enough to make a good hedge, and from the farmer's point of view are excellent plants for controlling erosion. They have a tendency to seed themselves and spread, but are not difficult to control. If you are in the areas where either will grow, I would certainly select at least one bush for your wildlife planting.

Holly and privet also furnish fall berries and make dense hedges for nesting cover or windbreak.

Most of the evergreen bushes and trees—spruces, hem-locks, firs, etc.—serve as excellent protective cover from snow and cold winds in wintertime. Plant them in rows or clumps. Small birds and mammals will seek the protection of their dense boughs.

If you have room for some of the small trees, the flowering dogwood not only has beautiful early spring blooms you can enjoy, but has fall berries for wildlife. The red cedar, chokecherry, crabapple, and mulberry are also good choices. (Plant mulberry trees a good distance from the house. That way, fallen ripe berries won't stain your walkways and drive-ways, or get tracked into the house. The mulberry is a super summer food tree, but it surely can be messy.)

The larger trees also offer many good choices. The red berry of the mountain ash is an excellent wildlife food. Many maples have small winged seeds in spring which are relished by birds, chipmunks, squirrels, and all kinds of critters. All oaks are great food trees, but they take time before they get big enough for their acorns to contribute much food. This is also true of the other nut trees, such as walnuts, pecans, and beech. But with all of these things time passes rapidly, and the sooner you plant, the sooner they will be producing.

Space your trees where they will have room to grow and spread out. Shrubs and small trees planted around them eventually will be in their shade, so choose those like dogwood that are shade tolerant. And remember to anticipate and leave plenty of open space for the grass-wild flower area and your lawn.

In the field of wildlife management there is a concept called "edge effect." This means that wild creatures nest and congregate along the edges of different habitats. You find more birds and mammals along the edges of a meadow than in the middle. More birds nest along the edge of a woods than in its center. In your planning, lay out your plantings so the edges wind around the center of the yard to get the maximum edge effect. The more edges you can create, the more attractive your yard will be to wildlife.

Plants for your plantings can frequently be obtained at bargain prices from state divisions of forestry. In fact, sometimes the plants are even given away if they are to be planted for wildlife.

In the state of Arkansas, for example, in late winter or early spring they have been giving away bundles of plants for wildlife plantings. These may contain white mulberry, black walnut, wild pecan, bicolor lespedeza, autumn olive, flowering dogwood, and others. In addition they also have made available seed packets, with sorghum, peas, and millet sufficient to plant a quarter acre.

Check with your state division of forestry, game commission, county extension agent, and soil conservation service to see if your state has plants available for wildlife plantings.

If you need still another argument to persuade your family to pitch in, tell them that not only will wildlife plantings benefit wildlife and make your yard more attractive, but they will give them more leisure time to enjoy other activities. Tell them why: The yard planted and maintained for wildlife has a smaller lawn to mow, requires little fertilizing and watering and no spraying, and seldom needs pruning or other care. It is a yard to be enjoyed both by members of the family and by the wild creatures.

◂4▸
Artificial Feeding

A rtificial feeding refers to the food you supply rather than that which grows or occurs naturally in the environment.

Sharing food with the birds is an old custom in Europe and in this country. One of our earliest naturalists, Henry David Thoreau, mentions scattering bits of corn, bread crumbs, and bits of food for the squirrels, rabbits, blue jays, chickadees, and other birds at Walden Pond in the 1840's.

Feeding this way has become important to the survival of migrating birds and many winter residents in the colder climates. Shorter days of winter mean less foraging time for the birds. In this season most of the wild seeds have been eaten, or they have dropped off the dead plants and been washed away by rain or covered by snow. The continuous search for food is a matter of life and death.

You can help a great deal by supplementing what the birds find on their own. A variety of foods may be used in feeding birds. Only by going over the lists of foods offered by successful bird feeders can you appreciate what a wide diversity of foods different birds like.

Here are just some of the foods that have been used to entice specific birds to the feeders: marshmallows, cranberries, mountain ash berries, sliced apples, suet, suet-and-seed mixtures, peanut butter, peanut hearts, walnuts, pecan bits, scratch feed, millet and canary seeds, raisins, thistle seeds, dates, grapes, oranges, peaches, plums, apricots, figs, scrambled and hard-boiled eggs, eggshells, popcorn, watermelon, cantaloupe seeds, banana, doughnuts, bread, rolled oats, sorghum grains such as kafir and milo, bits of meat, barley, cornbread, cracked dry dog food, hay chaff, cowpeas, cornflakes in milk, boiled potatoes, fresh raw fish, cooked spaghetti, piecrust, cottage cheese, cake, grape jelly, cooked squash, cooked rice, brown or white sugar, ears of corn, cherries, and sunflower seeds.

It's a long list. The only reason for going through it is to show you that the food list is limited only by your imagination and the taste of the birds in your area. Later in this chapter you will learn which birds are attracted to which foods. But most birds will come to your feeder for less exotic fare. However, to have a successful feeding program, foods must be chosen for the birds that are in your area, and they must be offered in a way that appeals to the birds.

Birds feed in what are called zones: Some birds will take only food offered on the ground. Some prefer low tablelike feeders. Others like similar feeders six feet above the ground. Many birds will not visit a feeder unless it is placed close to a heavy shrub to which they can fly if danger threatens. Woodpeckers visit various kinds of feeders, but prefer those that are along tree trunks or appear to be tree trunks. Goldfinches like hanging feeders with perches, where they are not bothered by larger birds.

This doesn't mean you have to do a great deal of study in order to feed birds. It does mean you must offer food in a suitable feeder correctly placed. It also means you should be observant and notice what foods the birds like and consume first.

I don't think it is necessary for you to learn the names of the various types of birds that visit your feeder, but chances are you will want to. For as those feathered strangers come and go, they are bound to stir your curiosity, and soon you will find yourself picking up the nearest bird book to identify a particular visitor. This is good, for which of us cannot benefit by learning a little more about the world around us?

As you learn which birds are visiting, and what they are eating, you will probably offer the food they most prefer and then begin adding new things to see what other birds you can attract. But the easiest way to get started feeding is by placing wild-bird seed mixture on a feeder and scattering some on the ground under it.

Numerous feeding studies have been carried out to find the food that most birds like. In general it is agreed that among the foods listed above, birds love sunflower seeds, and that they like cracked corn, millet, and nut meats. Wheat, sorghum grains, and barley grains were not as popular. Peanut butter is very popular with a great many birds.

While sunflower seeds are a top choice for your feeder, they are expensive. Most wild-bird grain mixtures have some in them, but the majority of the food consists of other grains. This is fine, for the sunflower seeds attract birds to your feeders, and most will eat other seeds when they are hungry.

There are reports of some feeders in the northeast feeding as much as fifty pounds of sunflower seeds a week when flocks of grosbeaks and other birds come in. At fifty cents or more a pound, you can see how expensive this would be. However, sunflower seeds are easy to grow. This is one way to increase your supply.

The family of sparrows and finches has over 70 species, and the majority will visit feeders. Cardinals, song sparrows, juncos, grosbeaks, and goldfinches are some of the best-known members of this seed-eating group. If you are trying to attract and aid a variety of birds, you have to choose foods that are economical as well as nutritious.

Let's consider foods you can offer at different feeding stations, feeders, or zones that will be most attractive and beneficial to the birds and most satisfying to you. Let's start with those birds that feed primarily on the ground. Quail, pheasants, mourning doves, ground doves, and brown thrashers eat only on the ground. In addition, cardinals, sparrows, red-winged blackbirds, grackles, towhees, and a host of others will eat on the ground as well as from feeders.

Scatter grains for these birds in an area where you can see who comes to your feeding area and where there is little grass. Choose a spot where you don't mind having a patch of bare earth. For as they feed, these birds scratch with their feet, moving leaves and other debris about, searching out the fallen seeds. After several months they will have removed the grass and small vegetation from this feeding area. I usually use an area under one of my regular feeders, so that any seed knocked off the higher feeder falls to the ground-feeding spot. That way it doesn't go to waste.

Choose either chicken scratch grain, which is a mixture of cracked corn and wheat, or one of the wild-bird grain mixtures for your ground-feeding spot. Ground feeders clean up wheat grains and milo that other birds don't enjoy. Scatter just the amount the birds seem to clean up in a day's time. In winter, feed in the same area. Just scatter the grain on the snow. If the snow is soft, the birds will scratch the seeds out; if the snow is hard, they will pick the grains off the top of the snow.

As a second feeding spot, choose an area where your feeder can be two to four feet off the ground and fairly close to a hedge or bush. A feeder in this location will attract sparrows, juncos, towhees, cardinals, chickadees, redwings, some of the warblers, and thrushes.

Offer the basic wild-bird grain mixture at this feeder too. If you want to attract the widest variety of birds, offer peanut butter-suet cakes as well. Suet is hard white beef fat. It can be obtained at the meat department of most food stores at a very low price—or perhaps for free, if you explain to the butcher what it is to be used for.

There are hundreds of formulas for making suet cakes. Basically, they are mixtures of suet with other ingredients that you hope will have appeal to birds and, even more important, that will be nutritious to them. Since peanut butter is very high on taste appeal, mix well one cup of chunky peanut butter with two cups of suet. Suet may be finely chopped or ground, or melted in a pan on the stove until it is soft enough to mix with peanut butter. In place of all or part of the suet, you can substitute congealed bacon grease or other fats saved from cooking. In addition to the basic peanut butter-suet mix there are many other foods that you can add to the basic mixture.

One of the best items is finely crushed eggshells. A couple of tablespoonsful will add needed calcium to the bird diet. A cup of oatmeal, cornflakes, or cornmeal can be mixed into the mixture to add variety and taste appeal, and to give it a drier consistency. Raisins, currants, bits of apple, and canary seed can be mixed into your concoction. Two other very good items that can be added are dry skim-milk powder and crushed bits of dry dog food. A cup of either or a mixture of both adds protein and makes it supernutritious for your birds.

Add what you wish and what you have available to the basic

Suet cake ingredients are placed in a muffin tin. Afterward they can be frozen and used individually.

peanut butter-suet mix, and then place the mixed material in a used milk carton, or in paper cups in a muffin tin. Refrigerate to chill and make firm. You can then cut the milk carton into slices, one for each daily feeding, or remove a muffin as needed (removing the container, which is not nutritious). Keep the balance refrigerated or frozen.

Peanut butter-suet cake will attract a variety of birds. It is popular with many of the warblers, woodpeckers, blue jays, chickadees, nuthatches, creepers, kinglets, and titmice. If you add currants and raisins and other fruits, you may even get bluebirds, robins, or mockingbirds to try it.

This peanut butter-suet mixture works fine in a homemade woodpecker feeder, and in pine cone feeders also (see p. 41). In fact, it can be used in almost every feeder to the advantage of the birds in your area.

In a feeder at the five- to six-foot height use the wild-bird grain mixture, bits of fruit, table scraps, and if possible some of your peanut butter-suet cake. This is a good feeder for experimenting with various foods if you wish to attract a large variety of birds, since a feeder at this height is attractive to many of the birds. Position it where you can readily see who is visiting.

One point to consider, if you wish to attract the greatest number of birds, is that types and numbers of birds will vary at different times of the year. In summer you have a resident bird population that nests, feeds young, and harvests whatever natural food is available. Many people do not feed birds in the summer, but we do. We feed wild-bird grain mixture all year round. In your area you may have blue jays, orioles, tanagers, catbirds, mockingbirds, bluebirds, and hummingbirds as summer residents. They may eat different foods from those the spring and fall migrating birds eat. These travelers appreciate and can use the nutrients you offer. And in winter, as birds shift southward, a different group moves in. Since the natural food of summer is dwindling, they very frequently can use help too. In the south we get the warblers and buntings. In the north redpolls, purple finches, and the grosbeaks are present.

While the basic bird grain mixture and peanut butter-suet cake will attract the majority in all seasons, there are specific foods you can use to attract some of the birds that won't feed on this basic diet.

Extra sunflower seeds will entice many of the migrating grosbeaks and finches to stay. This food is number one for attracting titmice, sparrows, nuthatches, chickadees, purple finches, and cardinals. To attract mockingbirds, use raisins, bits of apple, sliced orange or pear, grapes, and bananas, as well as peanut butter-suet cake. These same fruits will be attractive to robins, catbirds, bluebirds, thrushes, and waxwings. In fact, when cedar waxwings are migrating, a flock may eat ten to twelve apples daily. Finely chopped apples and nuts are attractive to many of the warblers. John Dennis, an authority on bird feeding, states that 38 of the 53 warblers can be enticed to a feeder if, through experimenting, you can find the key. Orioles and tanagers, and some warblers, have been coaxed to feeders by offers of grape jelly and other sweet fruit concoctions.

The red-bellied woodpeckers in our area eat bird grain at our feeders. They are also reported to like orange, apple, cracked corn, and pecan bits. Because it is expensive, we don't offer them such exotic fare. Flickers will sometimes come to feeders for meat scraps, orange sections, and apple bits. And even the large pileated woodpecker likes suet and cracked corn.

Tiny black thistle seed, which is usually called Niger seed, is attractive to goldfinches, pine siskins, and redpolls. It is usually fed in special hanging feeders which keep the seeds from blowing away. While it does attract birds, it is expensive, and therefore I cannot recommend it. Most of the birds that love Niger seed will come into your feeder for other foods as well.

I suggest these different foods if you want to attract a long list of birds. But regardless of what you feed, you will have better luck some years than others.

The birds themselves are not plentiful in certain years. Some years a mild winter and bountiful natural food sources may keep them from seeking out your feeders. Some years the birds don't migrate as far north or south as other years, though they always migrate to some extent. In other years some migrants may not come to your specific locale at all.

How deeply you get involved in a feeding program is not important, but what is important is that you get involved. Even if you just offer the birds a chance to clean up some of the leftovers from the family meals, they will appreciate it.

If you do start feeding a wild-bird grain mixture, there are a couple of points you should consider. First, it is much cheaper to buy your bird grain in 25- or 50-pound sacks. It can be obtained from feed stores and some grocery stores in large-size bags. Second, before you bring it home, get a metal garbage can with a metal lid to store it in. The 20- or 30-gallon size will hold 50 to 100 pounds of bird grain. It will stay fresh in a metal can, and squirrels and mice won't be able to chew holes in it. Squirrels riddled our plastic garbage cans and lids with holes until we switched to metal.

Before we leave this section, there are a couple of myths that should be put to rest. *You must not start a feeding program unless you can continue it indefinitely.* It is true that if food is available, more birds may be attracted to your yard, and some migrants may delay their departure. But unless they are trapped, the migrants can move south later, and what you have fed them will **make them** stronger for their journey.

If during winter you are going to be gone for a week or so, begin to prepare the birds by offering less and less food starting about ten days before your departure. This will force them to search out natural food sources in the area, and make them less dependent on you. Since they have eaten well up to now they will be better able to endure and forage. Even interrupted feeding is better than no feeding at all. But once you start, you should do it on a regular basis whenever possible.

It has been demonstrated many times that when abundant

natural food is available, the birds will desert your feeders and not be overly dependent on your feeding.

Another myth: *More predation occurs and diseases are spread among birds that congregate at feeders*. This has never been borne out in studies made by biologists and ornithologists at Cornell University.

Peanut butter kills birds. Peanut butter has been blamed for the deaths of some birds, since it was found in the mouths of a few dead birds at feeders. But it is agreed by professional ornithologists that peanut butter is an excellent food, both tasty and nutritious, and that it does not cause problems. The dead birds undoubtedly were weak. Chances are they were able to make it to the feeder but were beyond hope when they ate that last bite.

Artificial feeding of birds is not meant to be the main point in attracting birds and wildlife to your yard. It is just one more tool you have to help the wild creatures in your area. Natural foods, water, shelter and housing are all equally important. Artificial feeding is one way you get the satisfaction of seeing immediate benefits from your efforts.

·5·

Feeders for Wild Creatures

A feeder is a device to offer foods to birds and other creatures. There are feeders made of wood, wire, plastic, and glass. Some are as large as card tables, while others are as small as saucers. There are feeders designed for tiny seeds, medium seeds, large sunflower seeds, ears of corn, hunks of suet, and even for holding sugar syrup for hummingbirds.

In the appendix you will find a list of suppliers to whom you can write for catalogues and price lists, if you wish to buy a feeder. There is a wide variety in all price ranges to choose from.

I like to make my own feeders, and you might, too. You may enjoy building a feeder and having the lasting pleasure of seeing the birds use it daily. A homemade feeder is just as functional and efficient as a bought one. The birds will enjoy it no matter where it comes from.

Whether you make a feeder yourself or buy one, here are a few basic rules to remember. Wet seeds ferment, become moldy, and rot. Design your feeder so the seeds are not rained on. You can do this by making a roof on your feeder that is large enough to cover both the seeds and the feeding area. Or you can make a hopper or dispenser for the seeds that keeps them dry and protected.

Regardless of the pains you take to protect your seeds, a wild blowing rain will get the feeder and the seeds wet. When that happens, discard the wet seeds. Scatter them on the ground, where they will dry quickly and where the ground-feeding birds will make good use of them.

As a further precaution, provide feeders with drains. Flat tabletop feeders, with railings to confine the seeds, must have breaks in the railings to let the water out. Hanging-dish or bowl-type feeders should have small holes drilled in the bottoms to let any water out.

Another rule is to put up more than one feeder. You can start with one seed feeder. But chances are you will want to feed suet in the fall and winter, so add at least one suet feeder as well. As has been said, the ideal is to have several feeders in different locations and at different heights, in order to attract the widest variety of birds. This also keeps one bird from monopolizing a feeder.

If squirrels are a problem in your yard, adding guards to several feeders will keep the squirrels off. I am always amazed at the number of nice people who like birds and work to attract them, but who hate squirrels. Squirrels may be independent imps, but they are part of the wildlife population and should be tolerated and even provided for. Squirrels enjoy most of my feeders, and even though they steal many of the sunflower seeds, I like seeing them around. Of course, you can give them their own feeder and put squirrel guards on the rest.

To me, the best squirrel guards are a metal disk placed directly under the feeder or a section of stovepipe surrounding the support pole. The best disk for the purpose is the top of an

We enjoy and tolerate squirrels at our house, but they will visit and
monopolize most feeders unless you have attached squirrel guards.

old water heater. These can be obtained from any plumber or
plumbing supply shop. Old water heaters usually end up in
junkyards or landfill sites. Your neighborhood plumber will
probably be glad to save you a couple of tops if you explain

what they are for. However, water heaters vary a great deal in diameter. Be sure to ask for the widest possible top, for to be effective they must be at least 20 inches (50 cm) in diameter.

The stovepipe guard is slightly more expensive, since you must buy a 24-inch (60 cm) section of stovepipe, but it is even more effective. The stovepipe is placed over the top of the support pole and fastened to the bottom of the feeder, keeping an equal amount of space all around the pole. A squirrel climbing the pole enters the space between pole and pipe and is forced to turn around and leave when it finds a blind alley.

Some people apply auto lubricating grease or some other bizarre substance to feeder poles to keep the squirrels from climbing them. I do not recommend this practice. Not only can these substances make the squirrel sick, or even kill it if it licks itself clean, but the oily products are pollutants.

It is not difficult to build a tabletop feeder. You can do it in less than two hours. And the only tools you need are a drill, hammer, saw, and screwdriver. In Appendix III at the back of the book are step-by-step illustrated instructions to show you how to build and mount a feeder on a wooden pole.

If you wish to make a windowsill feeder, eliminate the squirrel guard and make the feeder just half the width. Use two screws to mount it on the windowsill. Most windows have wooden jambs on both sides to which you can anchor the feeder. If not, a hole can be drilled in the brick and a plastic shield placed in the hole which will accept and hold a screw.

To fill your feeder, just dump a pint or two of wild-bird grain mixture in the center of it, where it is protected by the roof. You can place suet or suet cakes near the seeds, or make a separate feeder for this food. A small mesh bag that once held onions, potatoes, or oranges makes a good suet feeder. Place apple-sized chunks of suet in it, and fasten it with a

A tabletop feeder is easy to build and is a very efficient way to feed wild-bird grain (directions on pages 127–133).

string to a convenient tree trunk. This will give woodpeckers a good base on which to perch when they feed.

You can make a slightly more durable suet feeder by bending a piece of hardware cloth or other wire mesh into a container shaped like a large tin can. Fasten it to a tree trunk. The openings in the wire mesh are large enough for the birds to get at the suet with their beaks.

An onion sack tied to a tree with string is a good way to feed suet.

To feed suet-peanut butter mixtures and the other foods described in the previous chapter, you can use a suet feeder or make a hanging log feeder. Choose a log 4 inches (10 cm) in diameter and cut it to a length of 24 inches (60 cm). With a large drill, make a dozen holes or pockets in the log. Place a hook in one end and hang the log from a convenient tree limb.

Fill the pockets or holes with peanut butter or a mixture of your choice. Woodpeckers, nuthatches, and chickadees will cling to your log feeder to enjoy lunch.

To make pine cone feeders, pour the melted suet-peanut butter mixture over pine cones, or stuff the mixture while it is still warm and soft into the crevices of the pine cones. When it is cool, tie string to the stems and hang each pine cone up as an individual feeder.

If you wish to make a feeder for the smaller birds, use the instructions in the appendix for making a feeder, but add one more step. Before you put the roof on, make a picket fence around the perimeter of the feeder with wooden rods. To make the fence, buy several ½-inch-diameter (1.25 cm) wooden dowel rods from the hardware store. Cut the dowel rods into 8-inch (20 cm) lengths. Drill ½-inch (1.25 cm) holes one inch (2.5 cm) apart around three sides of the feeder. Dip the dowel rods in wood glue one at a time and insert them into the holes. The rods will allow small birds to pass between them while excluding larger birds. It is a good idea to have one feeder for the small birds, since the larger birds may scare them away from the feeders without fences.

The fourth side should be a solid board that can be removed, so you can get into the feeder to fill and clean it when needed. Small hooks and eyes, obtained at the hardware store, can be used to fasten this solid panel to the corner roof-support posts.

Once you build your first feeder, you will have the confidence to try variations. The illustrations of feeders shown in books, catalogues, and magazines will spur you to design your own.

As I have already said, it's not difficult to make feeders. Convincing yourself to start one may be the hardest part of the whole project. Who knows, you may end up building them

Modify your feeder so that only small birds can use it by making a fence of dowels between which only they can fit.

and selling them to the people in your neighborhood. It would be a business venture which could help you and the birds.

But even if you build feeders just for your own satisfaction and for the birds in your yard, the results are worth the effort.

·6·

Water and Waterers

I f you provide water, one of the essential requirements
of all wildlife, it will naturally attract birds from the
surrounding areas and bring them to your yard. If the creatures
have already moved in, they will not have to leave your
sanctuary to find it once it is available.

How you provide water depends on where you live and your
desires. A concrete birdbath in the backyard is fine if you rinse
it thoroughly and fill it regularly with fresh clean water. Keep
several small blocks of wood floating in every birdbath. There
are good reasons for doing so. If the water freezes, the wood
blocks will help prevent the bath from cracking since the ice
will compress the wood instead of the concrete. Also, the
block provides a safe landing place for bees. Bees too need
water, and your blocks will help them to get to the water's
edge. If they fall in, they can climb out again on the blocks.

Better than the birdbath is a slowly dripping hose suspended
over a shallow bowl or a discarded garbage can lid. This is an
excellent way to provide water. It attracts birds like a magnet.
The garbage can lid need not be unsightly. It can be set into a

A fine spray fountain in a garbage can lid, a few rocks for perching, and landscaping, and you have a fine watering spot for wildlife.

shallow depression in the ground, so that it scarcely shows.

The drip should be slow, and gentle enough for the wild creatures to see and hear. Since you don't want to create a mudhole, a drip that just keeps the lid full is enough. It will replace the water that evaporates and that the birds take out. Today water is too expensive and too scarce to be wasted.

If you wish to conceal your source of water and to avoid the sight of a hose lying on the grass, bury a cheap garden hose or plastic tubing underground from your faucet to the lid. You can buy an adaptor at the hardware store with which to fasten the plastic tubing to the outdoor faucet. When you have dug a shallow trench four to six inches (10 to 15 cm) deep from the faucet to the lid, lay the hose or plastic tubing in it and cover it. Bring the end of the hose or tubing over the lid by tying it to a stake, and position it to drip into the lid.

Any excess water that spills or is splashed out by the birds usually soaks into the ground at once. This damp spot around the lid is an excellent spot to plant wild flowers that thrive in wet places. This will give a touch of color and beauty to that part of the yard. A few rocks placed near the lid for decoration and as bird perching spots complete your watering spot.

In winter, if the water freezes solid and the drip doesn't keep fresh water available and there are creatures about that need your water, you have several choices. An electric bird-bath heater doesn't cost too much and is inexpensive to operate. You can buy one at a garden supply store or order one from the suppliers listed in the appendix.

If the birdbath heater isn't a good choice for you, a cake pan or dish of warm water placed at your regular water site in the morning and late in the afternoon will give all the creatures a chance to get water for several hours at least twice a day before the water freezes.

Some folks build small concrete ponds with water-loving plants and recirculating waterfalls over rock slides. With colorful blooming water lilies and deep-green mossy rocks, the small pond becomes the beauty spot of the yard. It is worth considering as a family enterprise.

If you wish to build a concrete pond, there are only a few important considerations. First, the water must flow and not become stagnant. Stagnant water is not only uninviting, it can also be unhealthy. Bacteria grow rapidly in warm, slimy conditions. Some of these bacteria, such as those causing botulism, can cause diseases that can kill any creatures that drink the water. Either use a recirculating pump to carry the

WILDLIFE POND

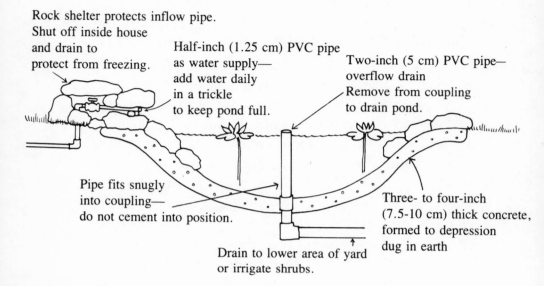

Rock shelter protects inflow pipe.
Shut off inside house
and drain to
protect from freezing.

Half-inch (1.25 cm) PVC pipe
as water supply—
add water daily
in a trickle
to keep pond full.

Two-inch (5 cm) PVC pipe—
overflow drain
Remove from coupling
to drain pond.

Pipe fits snugly
into coupling—
do not cement into position.

Three- to four-inch
(7.5-10 cm) thick concrete,
formed to depression
dug in earth

Drain to lower area of yard
or irrigate shrubs.

A wildlife pond can become the beauty spot of the whole yard.

water to the top of a rock slide, where it is aerated, or add fresh water regularly.

You can add fresh water with a hose timer fastened to your faucet. A hose timer is a clock-valve assembly. It allows water to flow to your pond only at the intervals you set on the clock. Timers can be purchased from suppliers listed in Appendix I.

Another good way to add fresh water is to use a small spray fountain attached to a hose. These may be purchased from garden supply stores or from the suppliers in the appendix. A spray fountain uses very little water. Place the fountain on a rock in the center of your pond.

Or you can arrange for a trickle from a plastic tube attached to the faucet. As long as the water stays fresh and moving, it will be beneficial to the wild creatures.

Provide some way to drain a concrete pond for cleaning, if this becomes necessary. Draining also protects the pond against cracking during freezing weather. However, if you make your pond shallow and saucer shaped, you don't need to drain it. Freeze cracking is usually not a problem, because as the ice expands it is forced out of the saucer.

On farms, ranches, and large homesites, a larger pond can be a water conservation device and a super attraction for wildlife. In Missouri, a study of 91 ponds showed that 90 species of birds and 10 species of mammals lived in the immediate vicinity of the average pond. It is a large undertaking. Not only would such a large pond involve the whole family, but you would also have to seek help from the soil conservation service and your county extension agent.

But as you can see, it doesn't require a pond or lake to supply your yard with water. Start with a plastic or metal garbage can lid and fill it regularly. Once you see how much the creatures in your yard use and enjoy it, you may wish to enlarge and add to this source of water by creating a more permanent pond to supply water all year long.

·7·

Birdhouses

Not all birds will use artificial houses or nests, but enough will do so to make this an important part of your program in attracting wildlife. Some of the birds that will appreciate the houses you provide are wrens, chickadees, titmice, nuthatches, tree swallows, bluebirds, flycatchers, purple martins, flickers and other woodpeckers, screech owls, barn owls, sparrow hawks, and wood ducks.

All of these birds normally seek out cavities in dead trees, protected corners of buildings, and other secluded protected spots. As you look about your neighborhood, you can see how few cavities and other suitable spots there are for these birds. Birds do not live or nest in many areas simply because no nest sites are available. Any house you provide is likely to be used the first season you put it up.

Before we consider building specific houses, here are some general rules to consider. A wide variety of birdhouses can be purchased from the suppliers listed in the appendix. But I am going to assume that you wish to build your own. For if you

Many smaller birds are attracted to your yard when housing is available. This house wren usually raises two families each year in this house.

can saw a board and nail two boards together, you can build most birdhouses.

Wood is the best building material for making birdhouses. All–metal houses, though better than nothing, usually get too hot in summer, and the treated waxed cardboard houses that are sold often don't last through a single nesting season. A wooden house will last from five to fifteen years, so it is well worth the time it takes to make a durable house.

The wood need not be expensive and smoothly planed, but can be any rough-cut lumber. Wood scraps around a housing construction site may provide a bountiful free supply if you ask the person in charge to save some of the smaller pieces for you. Wooden packing boxes, which stores discard, and discarded boards from neighborhood trash piles serve equally well. If you can't find any free source of lumber, buy any cheap unfinished or rough-cut lumber from your lumberyard. Most lumber stores carry low-grade inexpensive lumber that will be fine for your project.

Plan ahead and decide how many good spots for houses your yard sanctuary has, and exactly where they are. Most birds are attracted to houses placed four to fifteen feet above the ground. Place the houses so that they will receive shade at least part of the day, and so that the entrance opening faces away from the prevailing wind.

Design your houses with sloping roofs, so rain can run off. And put enough overhang on the roof to keep the rain from running into or being blown into the entrance hole.

Drill several small holes in the bottom board of the house, so any water that might get in can drain out.

Drill several ½-inch (1.25 cm) holes in the sides under the roof overhang to allow heat to escape and fresh air to come in.

Never make the entrance hole any larger than necessary to admit the bird you are trying to attract. For example, a hole ⅞ inches (2.2 cm) in diameter will admit wrens but will keep out sparrows. See the chart below. By selecting the proper size for the entrance hole, you make the house specific for certain birds. If you aren't sure what birds you can attract, or aren't sure what size entrance to make, vary the houses somewhat and let the birds around your home tell you which they like best by the houses they select. A house with an entrance not exactly correct is better than no house at all.

SPECIFICATIONS FOR BIRD HOUSES

Species	Floor of Cavity (in inches)	Depth of Cavity (in inches)	Entrance above Floor (in inches)	Diameter of Entrance (in inches)	Height above Ground (in feet)
Wren	4 × 4	6-8	4-6	⅞-1	6-10
Chickadee	4 × 4	8-10	6-8	1⅛	6-15
Titmouse	4 × 4	8-10	6-8	1¼	6-15
Nuthatch	4 × 4	8-10	6-8	1¼	12-20
Downy Woodpecker	4 × 4	8-12	6-8	1¼	5-20
Tree Swallows	5 × 5	6-8	4-6	1½	6-15
Bluebird	5 × 5	8-9	6-8	1½	3-10
Crested Flycatcher	5 × 5	8-10	6-8	1⁹⁄₁₆	8-20
Red-headed Woodpecker	6 × 6	12-15	9-12	2	12-20
Purple Martin	6 × 6	6	2	2	10-15
Robin, Barn Swallow, Phoebe, Song Sparrow	6 × 8	6-8	one or more sides open		8-12
Flicker	7 × 7	18	14	2½	6-20
Screech Owl	8 × 8	15	12	3	6-30
Wood Duck	10 × 12	24	15	3	5-20
Barn Owl	10 × 18	18	4-10	6	10-20

In general, bigger birds need larger houses. On the chart the recommended sizes for specific birds are given.

Always make your house so one side can be removed for cleaning purposes. At the end of each nesting session remove all old nest material and other debris. Usually mites and other insects will come out with the old nest material. That way the house is clean and will be ready for the next brood. If you find any creepy crawly insects in the house when you clean it, spray it with a rotenone-pyrethrum insect spray. The type of flea spray that is safe for use on cats is fine to use in your birdhouse. All spray will be gone long before spring nesting season comes around again.

Don't place birdhouses of the same size close together. Most birds are territorial and will drive away other birds of the same species from their nest area. For example, if you put four wren houses in a row, only one will be occupied, because the male wren will spend most of his time driving away all other wrens that come near. A wren house, however, can be close to a bluebird house, and a bluebird house can be near a flicker house. Different birds will nest together without a problem.

Choose spots for your houses that are as safe as possible from predators. A raccoon or foraging house cat can't reach a house hung from the eaves of your house. A snake usually won't invade a house on a pole six or seven feet off the ground. Hawks are less likely to harass smaller birds if the house is placed under the spreading limbs of a tree or partially concealed in the edge of shrubbery.

Houses for each type of bird are built in a similar fashion. Select from the chart on page 51 the dimensions of the finished house. Choose the materials you will need for your house and build it following the directions in Appendix IV, Building a Birdhouse. While those directions are for a bluebird house, you can modify them for the specific house you are building.

Your birdhouse can be painted or left to weather naturally. I prefer to paint the houses, because it makes them last longer. If you paint yours, choose light-green or -brown paint that blends into the background. Don't use a high-gloss paint, for birds don't like shiny surfaces, and don't paint the inside of the house. Put your house up in the fall, so all the paint odor is gone by spring nesting time.

If the floor below the entrance hole is smooth, rough it up to help the baby birds. This gives them toeholds when the time comes for them to climb out and leave the house. Use a chisel or a screwdriver to jab shallow holes in the wood below the nest hole. If you are using rough lumber, this step is not necessary.

When your house has been built, you will have to hang it. You can nail it to a post or a building, but don't nail it into a live tree. You might kill the tree that way. Instead, secure it to the tree with aluminum or other heavy metal clothesline wire. Thread the wire through the holes in your back panel and then pass it around the tree trunk or over a limb.

To keep the wire from cutting into the tree, fasten it loosely. You can further protect the tree by first threading the metal wire through a length of old rubber or plastic garden hose. The piece of hose should be long enough to keep the wire from touching the tree. As the tree grows, loosen or adjust the wire so it never cuts into the tree bark.

Fix your birdhouses firmly in position, for most birds won't use a house that swings back and forth in the breeze.

Starlings and sparrows are considered to be nuisance birds, and in some areas they will take over all your houses if you allow them to. One way to prevent this is by cutting or drilling the size of your entrance hole carefully. As the chart shows, a bluebird fits nicely through a hole 1½ inches (3.8 cm) in diameter. That's too small for a starling to get through. A great crested flycatcher, one of the species that badly needs housing, can fit through an entrance hole 1⁹⁄₁₆ inches (4 cm), which is also too small for the starling. But make the hole just ¹⁄₁₆ inch (.16 cm) larger and the starling can take over the house.

English sparrows like to live close to people. One way to thwart them is to place the houses they might choose away from your house. Choose a spot at the edge of a stand of trees and shrubbery at least fifty feet away from the house. Spar-

rows don't like high houses either. A birdhouse that is 12 feet
(3½ meters) high in a tree or higher frequently is not attractive
to sparrows. A low house 3 feet (1 meter) high is not attractive
to them either, but it will be more vulnerable to snakes and
other predators.

A few birds require specialized housing. Purple martins are
a good example. They prefer to nest in community groups or
colonies. To attract them you need to build a house that has
several separate nesting compartments.

This type of house is more difficult to build. It is a great
project for someone taking a wood shop course, or someone
who enjoys working with involved projects.

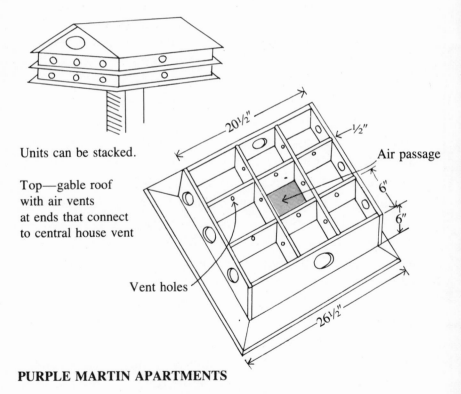

Units can be stacked.

Top—gable roof
with air vents
at ends that connect
to central house vent

Vent holes

Air passage

PURPLE MARTIN APARTMENTS

A purple martin house is more difficult to build, but worth the effort.

Our martins enjoyed our homemade martin house, but they also use a purchased metal house.

A further complication of providing for martins is that they prefer their house to be at least 10 to 15 feet (3 to 4½ meters) from the ground and at least 15 feet (4½ meters) away from any tree, building, or other structure. This means that if you build or purchase a martin house, you will need help to raise it into position.

We have a metal martin house that we bought, and also a home-built wooden one. The birds don't seem to prefer one to the other, but use both. We mounted ours on discarded telephone poles, and it was a job to get them up—and it is a job to clean them each year.

Baby wood ducks hatch in the security of their nest. They will be ready to leave after only one day.

Some people suspend clusters of gourds from poles for martin apartments. With 2-inch (5 cm) holes drilled in them they make fine homes. But since I have never used them I can't give you details on martin preference or size, nor how long they last.

Another bird that needs housing and has specialized requirements is the wood duck. From the chart you see that they

A baby wood duck in the entrance of its home

require large houses. For maximum baby survival the house should be situated near water, for mother and babies leave the nest the day after the eggs hatch. To help the babies climb out of the house, it's imperative that the wood of the wall below the entrance opening be roughened. After they jump out of the house, floating to the ground like dandelion puffs, the tiny babies follow Mother along the ground to the water. More babies will make it to the water if the journey isn't too long, and if there aren't too many obstacles to cross; so choose wood duck house sites with this in mind.

The entrance hole of a wood duck house should be just large enough for a mother wood duck to fit through, and small enough (let us hope) to exclude larger predators such as raccoons and wild cats. A hole 3 inches (7.6 cm) in diameter is adequate, although an elliptical hole 3 inches (7.6 cm) high and 3½ inches (8.9 cm) wide is better, because it is the shape of a duck's body.

If raccoons are a problem in your area, make or have made a shield and place it on the pole below your birdhouse to protect the nesting mother. Get a piece of thin galvanized steel from a sheet metal shop. They can cut it according to the sketch below, or you can do it yourself if you have the proper tools— heavy-duty tin snips and a cold chisel.

Nail three wooden blocks to the pole where you intend to place the shield. Form the shield into a cone shape and secure its edges with three short bolts and nuts. The blocks will keep the cone from sliding down the pole. A cone of this type provides protection from not only raccoons but snakes, mink, opossums, rats, and domestic and wild cats. (It is also a good idea for any type of birdhouse with a large entrance hole.) In many areas predators are so prevalent that you must install a cone to keep a wood duck house from becoming a death trap.

Providing housing for specialized birds such as martins and

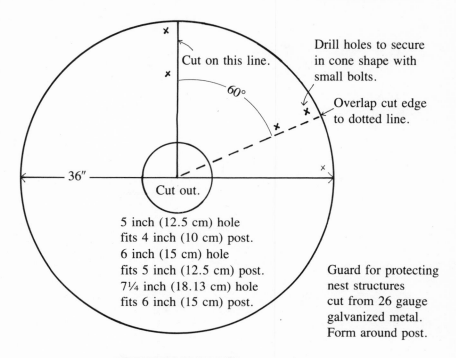

Cut on this line.

Drill holes to secure in cone shape with small bolts.

60°

Overlap cut edge to dotted line.

36"

Cut out.

5 inch (12.5 cm) hole
fits 4 inch (10 cm) post.
6 inch (15 cm) hole
fits 5 inch (12.5 cm) post.
7¼ inch (18.13 cm) hole
fits 6 inch (15 cm) post.

Guard for protecting nest structures cut from 26 gauge galvanized metal. Form around post.

PREDATOR GUARD

wood ducks is great, but it does require considerable effort. Don't try to leap in and provide houses for all birds right away. Build the houses you feel you can make. As you get more experienced, and if you find you enjoy seeing these creatures use the houses you provide, you can become more involved. There is a great satisfaction in knowing that baby wood ducks are hatching in the houses you have built, and that through your efforts wildlife has a chance to live.

Of course, things don't always work as planned. A little screech owl took over one of our wood duck houses. To her, this is her house, and she has raised a family in it for the past three years. No wood duck is fierce enough or brave enough to dislodge her from her adopted home. The only solution is to put up two or more wood duck houses.

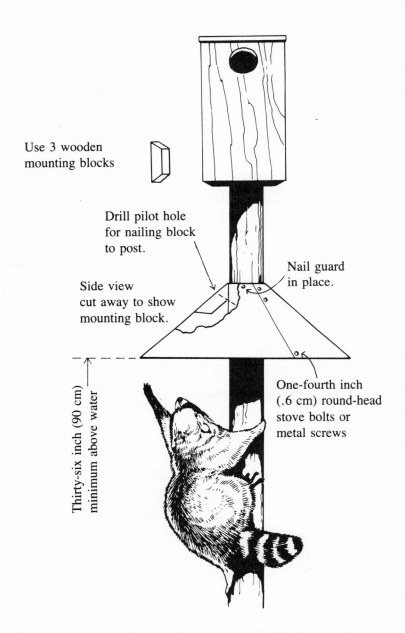

Use 3 wooden
mounting blocks

Drill pilot hole
for nailing block
to post.

Nail guard
in place.

Side view
cut away to show
mounting block.

Thirty-six inch (90 cm)
minimum above water

One-fourth inch
(.6 cm) round-head
stove bolts or
metal screws

A shield of galvanized metal on a pole keeps the wood duck house from
becoming a death trap.

Most birds prefer to gather and select their own nesting materials for their house. They gather bits of grass and tiny twigs, which they fashion into a nest inside the house. But others, such as wood ducks, do best if you place 2 to 3 inches (5–7 cm) of coarse sawdust in the nest box each winter before the spring nesting season.

Flickers prefer that you pack the house you make for them with sawdust. Removing the sawdust from the house apparently is part of the instinctive nesting procedure for them, similar to building a nesting cavity in soft dead wood. After they do this housekeeping chore, the house is much more suitable to them. Knowing specific habits of some of the various birds helps in providing materials they need.

Finally, some birds don't need complete houses, but use nesting platforms or shelves. While I have put platforms in the trees around our house, they have never been used. Robins, phoebes, and barn swallows, which use them, don't nest in Florida. So I stick to building the houses I've found our birds like.

You will have to do the same. Try the ideas I have given you and also those you read about elsewhere. Try ideas you come up with on your own. Find those things that work best for you, that satisfy the birds in your area, and that you enjoy doing. Even the simplest house will be needed by some creature in your yard, and you are the one to provide it.

•8•

Bluebirds

Eastern bluebirds require a separate chapter, for their story needs telling. I hope it will make you want to help them, for they are in need.

Since the late 1800's the number of eastern bluebirds has been steadily declining. At one time they were very common. Now most people under twenty have never seen one. The western bluebirds and mountain bluebirds are also in trouble and can also use help. But the situation of the eastern bluebird is critical.

The male bluebird is a beautiful blue color with a reddish breast. The female is not as colorful but is equally attractive. These gentle, beneficial birds consume great numbers of insects, and their song, a soft melody, adds to the joy of having them nearby.

In the last century the English sparrow and starling were introduced to this country. With their competitiveness and tremendous breeding capacity, they spread quickly throughout the east. As they did so, they drove the bluebirds from their

Starlings, here shown on a martin apartment, will also take over bluebird houses. Lack of homesites is the bluebird's most critical problem.

traditional nesting spots. The gentle bluebirds were no match for these aggressive invaders.

Bluebirds normally choose a hole in a wooden fence post or a dead tree in which to lay their eggs and raise their young. A nesting spot on the edge of an open meadow or grassy pasture is especially appealing to them. They usually select holes 3–10 feet (1–3.3 meters) above the ground and lay three to five eggs. The young birds are fed by both parents, and usually leave the nest when they are about 16 to 18 days old.

Usually trees that die are removed and fence posts that rot are replaced with metal posts, leaving bluebirds no nesting cavities. If the birds do find nesting spots or houses, they are frequently evicted or killed by the aggressive starling or forced out by scrappy sparrows.

Lawrence Zeleny, an author and retired scientist, is the man who deserves most credit for rescuing the bluebird. He believes that over 90 percent of the bluebirds were already gone by the time their plight was recognized around 1930 and the rescue started. His hobby and passion for the past fifty years has been helping bluebirds.

These birds don't need a lot of help—just a safe place to nest and raise their young.

A number of people are trying to help by building and maintaining bluebird houses. A proper house for bluebirds is one large enough for them to nest in and raise their young. It is also important that the entrance hole be large enough for bluebirds but too small for starlings. That's it. Providing secure nests has already started the bluebirds coming back in many areas of the country.

In Appendix IV you will find detailed instructions for building a bluebird house, as I have already said.

As usual, the material to use is wood, and it should be at least ¾ inch (1.9 cm) thick.

If you decide to paint the house, use light green or brown, and do your painting well before the nesting season. A white house may be cooler in summer, but bluebirds don't seem to choose bright houses that might attract attention. Dark-painted houses absorb too much heat if they are exposed to the sun. If the temperature inside goes above 110°F (44°C), eggs or baby birds are usually weakened or killed. When you put up your house, choose a spot where there will be shade part of the day.

When people put up a number of nest boxes for these birds,

it is called a bluebird trail. A trail may be only one or two houses or it can be several thousand. The history of some of these trails is interesting, and much of the important work has been done by youth organizations.

In 1959, a Canadian boys' club in Brandon, Manitoba—the Brandon Junior Birders—started a bluebird trail. They built houses and interested others in helping. Today that bluebird trail extends from Winnipeg to Saskatoon. There are over 7,000 bluebird houses along the trail, and 5,000 to 8,000 baby bluebirds fledge each year. Tree swallows also like the houses, and in 1976, when they were counted, over 15,000 baby swallows were raised along the trail. Swallows are not in the same danger as bluebirds, but they too can use help with houses.

The Youth Conservation Corps in South Carolina built 700 bluebird houses in 1979. These were distributed by Boy Scout troops that took the responsibility for setting them up in proper spots. These houses were put up with sponsorship of the South Carolina Garden Clubs. Driving along Interstate 26 through South Carolina, you can see bluebird houses for 200 miles from the North Carolina border southward past the state capital, Columbia.

Fifth and sixth graders from Bridgeforth Middle School in Pulaski, Tennessee, built 400 bluebird houses in 1979 and over 200 in 1980. These young people take the houses home and put them out around their yards.

Unfortunately, bluebirds won't nest in urban areas. They need quiet and open surroundings. But don't let this keep you from helping them. Bluebirds like nesting along golf courses and the edges of cemeteries, in state and city parks, and along country roadways. Ask permission, and the owners of most of these places will be happy to allow you to put up one or more bluebird houses.

In Delaware State Park, 29 miles north of Columbus, Ohio, the first bluebird houses were put up in 1977. One pair of bluebirds nested in 1978. In 1979 there were 66 boxes, and 7 pairs raised 44 bluebirds. In 1980 90 boxes were set up for the returning birds in the open areas of the 7,411-acre state park.

While this is great, and the birds are showing that they can come back, they still need your help. A severe winter or prolonged cold spell in spring will kill many of them—they freeze or starve to death. In addition, natural predators such as snakes, raccoons, and house cats do their best to cut down the survivors.

In the open meadowlike areas that bluebirds like for nesting homesites, they can also find insects to feed themselves and their babies. It's best to pick a spot 3–5 feet (1 to 1½ meters) above ground level and securely fasten the house to a post or tree. Sparrows sometimes take over the houses. Some bluebird fanciers believe that if the house is placed 3 feet (1 meter) above the ground, the sparrows won't consider the house, since they prefer nesting higher. Since there are no sparrows in my area, I like to put the house at my eye level. That makes it easier to check on the nesting birds, and certainly makes it easier to clean out the house.

Mount the house so that the entrance faces away from the prevailing winds to keep rain from blowing in, and try to choose a spot where there is a tree or shrubbery 15–25 feet (5–8 meters) away. When young birds leave the nest they will fly to this spot.

The birdhouse must be cleaned out as soon as the young birds leave the nest. If you do this, the adult birds will usually use the nest box again and raise another family in the same year. These birds will seldom use a dirty house.

It is much easier to clean out the house if you can open the whole front or side. A removable roof makes the job more difficult, because it's hard to gather up all the little bits and lift them out. It's simpler to just open the side and sweep everything out with your hand in one motion.

If your bluebird nest box has been occupied, and you find it empty and see bits of nest material hanging from the entrance hole, chances are a raccoon has climbed up and reached into the house, killing and eating mother and babies. You can thwart raccoons in three ways.

One way is to make a second entrance hole in a board about 1½ inches (3.8 cm) thick and four inches (10 cm) square. Nail the board over the existing entrance hole, so the two holes are lined up with each other. This makes the entrance hole into a tunnel that a raccoon has difficulty reaching through.

In addition, if raccoons are a problem where you live, make the entrance hole higher above the floor, so the raccoon has difficulty reaching the babies. Finally, if you mount your houses on posts you can make predator guards, as described on p. 58. This is an added expense, but it will keep out raccoons and is the only effective way to exclude snakes that may be robbing the nests.

I don't believe in killing the raccoons and snakes. Raccoons have a place in nature's world, and certainly anyone with a knowledge of snake behavior must agree that they are beneficial. As I have already said, I do not believe in smearing the post with auto grease. It doesn't work, and it can make the wild creatures sick if they eat it while cleaning themselves. It is much more practical in the long run to try to outmaneuver the creatures that interfere with the ones you wish to help.

Try to monitor your houses at least once a week during the nesting season. Bluebirds usually start nesting in April. They frequently raise a second clutch—that is, batch of babies—in June, and sometimes a third in August. Sit where you have a good view of one or more houses and keep a watch for thirty minutes. See if bluebirds are visiting the houses. Are they just inspecting? Are they carrying nesting material? Are they carrying insects to feed young birds? Number each house you have and keep notes on each observation. At the end of each observation period take a quick peek inside the house. Are there eggs? How many? Are there babies, and how many? While you watch, you may see the female leaving the nest with bits of eggshell. This means babies are hatching. Make a note of the hatching date, and then see how long before the young birds leave. It is usually sixteen to eighteen days from hatching to fledging. If your babies are gone in seven days, you know something got them. What started as a nesting success has become a catastrophe.

Keeping such records is not absolutely necessary, but it can be interesting. You may wish to keep track of your efforts to help bluebirds recover. The important thing is that you put up a house and help. If you begin to see an increase in bluebirds around your home, and each season more of your houses are being used, you have some assurance that your efforts are paying off and that locally the bluebird is coming back. It would be a help if you forwarded your observations to the North American Bluebird Society, P.O. Box 6295, Silver Springs, MD 20906, so your results can be correlated with the results of others engaged in the same activity. That way national and state trends can be charted.

The book *The Bluebird, How You Can Help its Fight for Survival*, by Dr. Lawrence Zeleny, $5.50 per copy postpaid, is available from the same organization. It gives a great deal more specific information on bluebird habits, behavior, and interesting stories about these birds.

Dr. Zeleny has eleven rules for those who would put up bluebird houses. Although I have already gone over most of them, I'll list them for you. Though they differ slightly from my suggestions, they are the standard rules which have helped hundreds of bluebird fanciers.

1. Select good habitat. Open country with scattered trees or low, sparse cover is best.
2. Avoid brush and heavily wooded areas. This is the domain of the house wren.
3. Avoid areas where house sparrows are abundant.
4. Avoid areas of extensive pesticide use.
5. Mount nesting boxes three or more feet from the ground, preferably on poles.
6. Face box in any direction, but preferably toward a tree 25–100 feet distant.
7. Because of bluebird territorial preference, keep boxes at least 100 yards apart.
8. Protect boxes against snakes, raccoons, and other predators when necessary.
9. Monitor the boxes about once a week during nesting season, if possible.
10. Always remove house sparrow nests immediately when found. Remove bluebird and other nests as soon as the young birds have flown.
11. Inspect boxes in winter. Clean and repair if necessary.

The rules have been formulated by Dr. Zeleny over a long period of working with and helping bluebirds. When he retired and started a new trail with thirteen houses in 1967, the bluebirds raised about 20 young birds. By 1970 his trail in Maryland had 52 houses, and over 200 young bluebirds had fledged. Each year since that time about the same number of baby bluebirds joins the bluebird population, replacing those which have been lost for various reasons and, we hope, giving us a net gain in numbers.

Even a single house can be important to bluebirds in your area. Many bluebirds stay where they nested during the winter months if food is available. They feed on berries, rose hips, sumac, and other plants. Any of the natural food plants you start in your sanctuary will help the bluebirds make it through the winter. This is another way you can help.

Your efforts are important. Dr. Zeleny closes his book with this thought: "The lives of people helping the bluebirds are enriched by the realization that they are doing something tangible to help a lovely form of life survive. The same satisfaction can be yours. Bluebird conservation is a task that cannot be accomplished by law, edict, oratory, or armchair philosophy. It can be accomplished only through broad and active public participation. The cost is small but the reward is great."

‹9›

Hummingbirds

Everyone who sees a hummingbird fly in to eat at our feeder, and watches it hover for a moment and then gently move into a feeding position, invariably exclaims, "It moves like a helicopter!" And indeed they do. To hover, these tiny birds move their wings not up and down like most birds, but backward and forward, describing a figure eight. Not only can they hover, they can fly backward, and even upside down.

When this first spurt of intense fascination with the aerobatics of these feathered jewels begins to fade, it is replaced by a desire to know more about these "glittering fragments of the rainbow," as Audubon called them. While it would take a large book to cover the specifics of the over 320 species in the western hemisphere, some basic information is in order if you wish to attract them to your yard.

Hummingbirds breed and nest in all states in the continental United States, even as far north as southern Alaska, and much of Canada. Only one species, the ruby-throated hummingbird, is found east of the Mississippi River. California, Arizona, and other states in the southwest have the greatest variety of

A hummingbird coming to the feeder hovers, like a helicopter.

hummers. In spring and summer thirteen species or more live in this region. A few species stay in southern California to spend the winter, but the majority of the hummingbirds in the United States migrate to Central and South America.

The eastern ruby-throated males usually leave in late August, while the females follow in September. They migrate to the Yucatan, southern Mexico, and as far south as Brazil.

Think if it—this tiny mite that weighs only 2.5 to 4 grams flies from the eastern half of the United States all the way across the Gulf of Mexico in the fall.

They return in the spring, moving northward as warm April breezes push back the cold, flowers begin to bloom and insects emerge from their dormant states. These tiny birds live primarily on insects and on the nectar they gather from the flowers. Their long beaks are adapted to reach to the base of flowers, where the nectar collects. However, it is estimated that a major portion of their diet is insects.

They can catch and devour fruit flies and other small flying insects on the wing, deftly snatching them out of the air. They will pick off spiders, flies that are eating, and other sitting insects, but they prefer flying insects. They also constantly visit flowers in their area for sips of nectar.

Hummingbirds spend most of their daylight hours feeding. In one study hummers in large individual cages were observed for sixteen hours. During this period each bird averaged 267 trips to its feeder for nectar, and consumed an average of 677 fruit flies. It has been said that if the average man, who normally eats 2½ pounds of food a day, ate like a humming-bird, he would eat 200 pounds (91 kg) of food daily.

Hummers use up great amounts of energy. With a body temperature of 105°F (41°C) and high metabolic rate, they need a large amount of carbohydrates and have an oxygen requirement twenty times ours on a weight basis. The act of flying consumes a great deal of energy, with wing strokes of 25–200 per *second*. That is what gives the wings a blurry appearance when you see hummers flying near a feeder.

The wings' pushing against the air at such a rapid rate causes the humming noise we associate with these birds. After you get accustomed to them at your feeders, you hear them before you see them. Without looking up, you can say, ''The

A hummer may visit hundreds of flowers daily for a tiny drop of nectar from each.

hummer is back,'' then you turn to watch with fascination as it perches on your feeder and begins to eat. Hummers may also land on small tree branches to rest and lounge. But you won't find them walking about on the ground, for their tiny legs are not adapted for running, climbing, jumping, or even walking. But then, if we could fly as well as they do, we wouldn't need to walk either.

The female hummingbird builds a tiny nest, and lays and incubates two to four eggs. She raises the young birds without assistance from the male. In a couple of weeks the babies are flying about visiting flowers and feeders on their own.

A unique characteristic of hummers is their lack of fear of humans. They willingly accept and enjoy the feeders that are put out for them. Many of the suppliers listed in the appendix have inexpensive hummingbird feeders in their catalogues. If you are interested in attracting this bird, you might buy your first feeder in order to get an idea of how it works. When hummingbirds begin using it, you can consider making additional feeders yourself.

You will notice several things about the feeder you purchase. First, it has an abundance of red plastic flowers and trim. Hummingbirds are attracted to red. Also, it will probably come with a set of instructions for making syrup. When the birds investigate your red feeder, they find openings where they can sip the syrup you have provided for them. Do not add red coloring to the syrup. It is the color of the feeder that attracts the birds.

You can make syrup by mixing one cup of sugar with three cups of water. Boil the water first to kill any bacteria that might be in it. When the mixture cools, fill your feeder and store the remainder in a clean jar in the refrigerator. Use this to refill your feeder as needed.

You can also use honey. Some people consider honey to be more nutritious for the birds. It is more easily digested. Because it can become moldy in a neglected feeder, some bird feeders do not recommend using honey syrup. But it is still the basic ingredient of choice in many formulas used by zoos for their hummingbirds.

The mixture is the same, one part honey and three parts water. Again boil the water, then mix the honey into the water when it is cool. Store it in your refrigerator. Empty any syrup not consumed by the birds every other day, and thoroughly clean your feeder before refilling.

Even sugar syrup can become moldy, so all feeders must be cleaned at least once a week, or more often if needed. When you clean your feeder, discard any syrup remaining and rinse thoroughly with hot water several times. If a film remains on the inside of the feeder, use a baby bottle brush and a dilute vinegar-and-water solution to scrub the inside of the feeder. It will usually dissolve any remaining film. Rinse again and then refill your feeder. Do not use any detergents, since the residue may make the birds sick.

It is not a lot of work to set up a couple of feeders, and the enjoyment of watching the hummers is most rewarding.

Once you see how feeders are made—use your imagination and make your own. Any jar with a slender neck opening can be made into one. Find a cork to fit and make a hole in the cork for a short piece of flexible plastic tubing. The birds will suck the syrup out on their long barbed tongues. Use red ribbon or plastic as color in the area of the cork.

Attach a wire to the hook on your feeder and hang it where it will be in the shade most of the day. A little sun is fine, but all day in the sun will stimulate mold and fungus growth in the syrup. It does not matter if the feeder swings—flowers sway and swing in the breeze, too.

It's a good idea to hang your feeder where someone in the house can see it during most of the day. Then you will know when the hummers start using the feeder. Hummers do considerably more feeding early in the morning and just at dusk, so watch for them at these times. Frequently you will hear them chirping happily as they flit up to the feeder.

One thing to watch for is a single bird taking possession of the feeder. A little flying tiger will decide that your feeder is his feeder and his alone. In that case, he will spend his time chasing away other birds that dare to trespass near his feeder. The only remedy is to put up another feeder, preferably where the little rascal can't see it, or he will try to protect the second feeder, too.

Regardless of whether you use homemade or purchased feeders, hang them out in April or May when the hummers are due back. Keep them clean and filled until the birds leave in September. You will know when they are gone, for you will miss their happy chatter.

Insects may be attracted to your feeders. Bees are said to take over some feeders. Bee guards are available for some feeders, and our hummers quickly got used to them, although we never had a bee problem even though we have two hives close by. Ants, too, can be a problem. When ants or bees find a feeder, I usually just move it to a new location. The hummers will seek it out. Some say that you can smear a little salad oil or Vaseline on the wire that holds the feeder in place, and that this will discourage the ants. But I have never tried this.

To help attract hummers, you can plant the flowers that they enjoy. They like jewelweed, trumpet honeysuckle, gladiolus, petunia, fuchsia, columbine, nasturtium, penstemon, hollyhock, morning glory, geranium, hibiscus, evening primrose, and a host of other flowers.

But the primary way to attract hummers is with feeders. As an added bonus, when you put up hummingbird feeders, you frequently attract other birds. Woodpeckers, titmice, nuthatches, thrushes, warblers, orioles, tanagers, and finches have been seen sipping from the feeders from time to time.

There's one last point you should be aware of. Hummers can go into a state of suspended animation or hibernation to reduce energy needs. At night or while resting in cold weather, a hummingbird will fluff out its feathers, close its eyes, and go into a deep sleep. Its body temperature drops as its heart rate slows. All body systems slow to conserve needed energy. On waking, the hummer's heart speeds back up and the bird begins functioning normally.

An exhausted hummingbird with depleted food reserves sinks into an inactive state that resembles a coma. If there is no food reserve for energy that the bird can mobilize, it dies. Sometimes you can revive a bird if you find it in this comatose state.

Last summer a little hummer invaded my workshop. It flew in through the door. I don't know how long it had been flying about from window to window looking for a way out, but I walked in just as it collapsed into the sink below a window. As I picked up the apparently lifeless bird, I realized for the first time just how tiny they are. I could scarcely even feel it lying there in the palm of my hand. As I scrutinized it, I was surprised to see one eye open slowly. The bird looked at me but didn't try to move.

I carried it out of my shop to the porch where the feeders hang. Carefully holding it so as not to squeeze its chest and interfere with what little breathing it was doing, I dipped its beak into the syrup in the feeder. There was no reaction or response. In a few minutes I did it again. Still no reaction. Again I dipped the beak, and this time I carefully opened the beak a tiny bit with my fingers, so the drop of syrup hanging on its tip went into the mouth. No reaction.

A few minutes later, when I dipped the beak again, I saw the hummer's tongue emerge to bring the syrup from the beak into its mouth. Eight or ten successful dips later the little bird opened both eyes and cocked its head to look at me. After it was satisfied with its examination, it closed its eyes again while I lifted it back and forth to the feeder. Three or four minutes later it righted itself in my hand, sat up, looked at me again, and fluttered its wings for three or four seconds. Then it allowed me to lift it up to the feeder for six or eight more trips.

As I lowered my hand from the feeder the tiny bird sat up, looked at me, fluffed up its feathers and shook—straightening them out—then opened its wings and began to move them up and down. Faster and faster it moved them, until the familiar humming sound came from the tiny bird in my hand. After five seconds of warm-up flight the little helicopter slowly lifted up from my palm, rose six inches, hovered again, gave me one final look, and then zipped off upward, vanishing over the trees.

The little hummer never said thank you for its rescue. But it didn't need to, for the satisfaction I felt made me feel good all day long.

·10·
Attracting Mammals to Your Yard

When you start a sanctuary in your yard, mammals as well as birds will be attracted to it. The same plantings that furnish food and sites for birds offer food and cover for mammals. The feeders you stock with seeds will also draw mammals.

The first and most obvious group to move in will be the squirrels. The eastern gray squirrel will appear like magic and make itself at home. The others are shyer, but they too can be attracted. The next chapter will cover the different types of squirrels in detail.

Chipmunks of various species are a normal inhabitant over much of the country, and they too will quickly find your sanctuary. Almost everyone enjoys watching these cute striped varmints scurrying around. When they aren't harassed, they become quite tame and soon learn to visit feeders and to coax you for a handout. When you provide the protection of a substantial rock pile, or see that their tunnel entrances under a big tree are not damaged, they move in, breed, and take over the yard.

They are good climbers, and unless your feeders have squirrel guards on them, the chippers will eat all the seeds they can hold and even go on to stuff their cheek pouches full. They carry the extra to the storeroom in their burrow. When a half dozen chipmunks are willing to work all day carrying off the seeds from your feeder, you can see why some people who feed birds detest chipmunks. But I can never understand why these people, rather than shooting, poisoning, or trapping them, don't put squirrel-predator guards on their feeders. That way everyone can live happily together. The chipmunks then harvest seeds and berries from your plantings just as they do in the wild.

The next most obvious visitor will be the rabbit. Rabbits ask for little more than a safe spot to hide in during the daylight hours. At dusk they leave their hideout to play, explore, feed, and forage. They feed until daylight, then seek out shelter again. You can do more than just provide a spot to hide—you can provide a safe daytime sanctuary.

One of the best sanctuaries for rabbits is a brush pile. Collect branches, trimmings, and prunings from your own yard and your neighbors'. Stack them in a secluded corner of your yard. The rabbits will find the pile and make nest spots and tunnels through it. Here they can hide, and if pursued can elude larger predators like house cats or foxes.

If you have space, create several piles and add to them each year, so they remain as a sanctuary for the rabbits in your yard. You can also plant a patch of rosebushes or blackberry bushes. The sharp thorns on these bushes are no hazard to the bunny that slips through their protecting stems, but they slow up or stop more predators.

A bountiful supply of food is always present for rabbits, for they eat almost everything green. But they seem to enjoy most of all the same vegetables that we enjoy. This means you have to fence your garden if the rabbits become plentiful. If you want to stay on good terms with your neighbors who garden, offer to fence theirs, too. At hardware stores you can buy chicken wire in rolls 18–24 inches (45–60 cm) high. This material is not expensive and will fence out any troublesome rabbits. Pound short stakes into the ground at 8–12- foot (2½–4 meter) intervals around the garden and stretch the wire around them. The wire is low enough for you to step over to get into the garden.

It's enjoyable to walk out early in the morning and see a rabbit skipping across the lawn, or to sit quietly at dusk and watch young rabbits at play together. Fencing the garden is a small price to pay for this enjoyment.

Other mammals are less visible. Mice will move in when there is shelter in heavy grass, or if other cover is available. They find weed seeds and other things to eat, but they also enjoy the bird grain that falls to the ground around your feeders. In fact, unless you keep your bird grain in securely closed metal containers, they will eat through feed sacks and help themselves to the grain.

Rats too will be attracted to feed not properly secured in metal containers. When filling containers from your bulk bird grain, don't spill any. It takes just a little grain spilled each day to encourage rats and mice to move into your food storage area.

Mice are a normal part of the environment in any woodland community. I enjoy seeing them and think they are attractive, but of more importance to the wild community is the fact that they are a primary food souce for hawks, owls, fox and many other creatures. Do away with all the mouse families and you do away with their dependent predators.

Rabbits are enjoyable. A little lettuce from the garden is a good trade-off for their presence.

Rats are not considered desirable. They do great damage and cause many dollars' worth of destruction to stored food grains on farms. The best way to keep from having them move into your buildings is to make sure there is no food available for them. Spilled grain and feed containers that are not rat proof invite rats to come live with you.

There are woodland rats—kangaroo rats, cotton rats, and others that don't move in with people. My prejudice doesn't extend to them, and they are welcome to set up homes in the cover of the overgrown yard areas. They too serve as food for many predators and are a normal part of the environment.

Opossums, skunks, and raccoons will also move in where there is food and shelter. Opossums and skunks choose homes under lumber piles and buildings, and in culverts, trash-littered sheds, and hollow logs. The best way to keep them from moving in with you is to be certain they can't get in under your buildings, porches, or sheds. Keep things picked up and clean, so they can't find a place to set up housekeeping in your buildings. You can nail four boards together to make a hollow den, or place a board on rocks or bricks. Then they will find a place in a wooded part of your sanctuary. You will see them come and go, but they *won't* become obnoxious by moving in with you.

The raccoons can be a special problem. They are intelligent, amusing, adaptable rascals. We enjoy having them around, but they will take over your house and yard unless you out-maneuver them. They normally live in nests they fashion in hollow trees. You can fix a nest box for one high in one of your largest trees. Make the dimensions of the house 1 foot square (30 cm) and 3 feet (1 meter) deep, with an entrance hole 6 inches (15 cm) in diameter. Construct it out of wood just as you would a birdhouse. Hang it close to the tree trunk, with the entrance of the house facing away from the prevailing winds, at least 20 feet (7 meters) above the ground.

Raccoons are solitary creatures. They don't join one another for company, except during the mating season. They are also territorial. If one raccoon moves into your yard and into the

The white-faced mouse, a gentle, attractive mouse, is found over most of the U.S.

house you have made, it drives off all other raccoons. For this reason one raccoon is about all you can expect to live in your sanctuary—and even that may be one too many.

In urban and suburban settings raccoons soon learn to open and dump garbage cans to find choice food tidbits. Make a bin with a heavy wooden lid in which to store your garbage cans. Or you can stop the raccoons from opening the cans by placing elastic cord across the lid of the can and fastening it to the handles on each side with hooks. These cords may be bought at any hardware store. Of course, your neighbors may not appreciate being forced to do this with their garbage can every night. You may get the brunt of the blame for encouraging raccoons to come live in your neighborhood.

At our house we have raised quite a few orphan baby raccoons. When these babies were adapting and learning to be wild raccoons, we had to put out food for them until they learned to find food on their own. We set up a hopper-type feeder close to the ground at the edge of the woods. We filled it with chunks of dry dog food each evening. At dusk the parade of raccoons and other creatures would start.

I fixed a bell on the feeder and a red colored spotlight on the house. We could turn the light on from inside the house to see who was visiting the feeder when we heard the bell tinkle. Wild creatures ignored the red light.

All night long there would be a parade. Mother raccoons would come with four or five babies. When they left, other single raccoons would follow. While raccoons are territorial, the feeder was neutral ground. There was no fighting so long as each waited till the one at the feeder was finished and left before the next one approached. If two arrived at the same time, the growling and fighting was noisy until the loser moved into the darkness or up a tree until the victor satisfied its hunger.

A feeder for mammals in a secluded portion of the yard. Dry dog food is offered each evening. The fence wire keeps deer and dogs out but lets raccoons, opossums, and foxes through easily.

In the nightly parade we also had opossums, red fox, gray fox, and feral house cats regularly visit the feeder. None of these caused us too much trouble, but we did have to take certain precautions.

Since we kept chickens, the hen house had to be locked at night, or our chickens would have been killed and carried off one by one. All grains and bulk dog food had to be kept in metal cans with lids that fit well. Our garbage cans were kept in a metal rack, so they couldn't be turned over. And all the ventilating areas to the attic of our house had to be covered with hardware cloth after the raccoons decided they would rather live in our attic than in the woods.

They climbed trees near the house and got on the roof. Then they tore out the regular screen material. You could hear the rip of screen at dawn, and then the clumping around on the ceiling as they wandered around choosing their beds for their daytime sleep. When they left at night, I had to fix the holes so they couldn't get back in. We played this game until I finally replaced all the screen material with the heavy hardware cloth they couldn't tear out.

Yet even with these minor problems, I enjoyed having the raccoons around. We shared the sweet corn in our garden with them. I don't think our family would trade anything for the enjoyment of watching a raccoon family on its first outing, but then we don't have close neighbors either.

The problems presented by raccoons apply to deer, too. We have raised several fawns. We turned a couple loose on a ranch not too far away, and two more we let loose here at the house. They weren't tame, but they weren't terrified of humans either. They enjoyed visiting the gardens on their wanderings within a half-mile radius of their new home. Needless to say, the owners of the gardens didn't like it very much. One person called me several times and wanted me to get my deer out of

Semitame raccoons are unafraid of people and can be a problem, for they get into everything. In spite of this we have enjoyed them.

his garden. When I explained that they weren't my deer, but wild deer I had raised for the State of Florida, and that I had no way of catching them, I was assured that since I couldn't take care of the problem, they would. I have every reason to believe two of the deer were killed by angry gardeners.

Naturally I feel guilty for having raised these deer to accept people, and you face the same problem if you attract deer or other wild animals to your yard. Frequently, they will become tame enough not to fear humans.

As you can see, attracting some of these mammals to your yard can cause trouble as well as bring great personal enjoyment. You have to weigh all the factors and then decide whether you wish to actively encourage them by building shelters and placing feeders out with dog food in them, or to just let these creatures seek and find their own niche in the environment you have created.

·11·

Squirrels and More Squirrels

Across the country there are primarily four types of squirrels that will be attracted to your yard and to your feeder. The eastern gray squirrel is the most common. It is found throughout the east and as far west as Texas, Oklahoma, Colorado, and northward. It is the squirrel most people are familiar with.

The fox squirrel is a larger squirrel with a bushy tail like a fox's. It is found in the same area, but is much shyer than the gray squirrel. It will visit feeders when it learns that it will not be harassed. It is not nearly as common as the gray squirrel, and has not adapted to urban living as the gray squirrel has.

The flying squirrel is quite common. It doesn't really fly but glides. This big-eyed nocturnal squirrel has a web of skin that connects the front and rear legs to each other. When it glides, it stretches out its legs, which makes its body wide and flat. When it leaps into space, this skin creates a crude airfoil that gives it some support as it sails to the next tree.

There are two species of flying squirrels, the southern flying squirrel and the northern flying squirrel. Between them they

91

cover much the same area as the gray squirrel, but the larger, northern, species covers most of Canada and even portions of Alaska. You probably have them living near you, but they are so shy that most people never see them.

The northern woodland, the Rocky Mountains, and the western coastal areas are red squirrel country. There are numerous species, but most of these small reddish squirrels are similar in appearance. They are solitary, territorial individualists, but they quickly learn to accept food from people.

There are other species of squirrels, but they are not common and are not found over large areas of the country, nor do they usually live near people.

Since the eastern gray squirrel is most common, let's consider it first. You don't have to work to attract it. Offer it a little food, and it will move in and build its own nest of twigs and leaves near the top of the tallest tree.

Many people who feed birds dislike the gray squirrel, because it isn't satisfied with just a little food. Once it finds your unprotected feeder, it will sit right in the middle of it, driving off any birds that dare to approach, and eat the choice sunflower seeds. When it has eaten all it can hold, it may leave the feeder for a short nap, but its place will only be taken by another squirrel.

If you don't want squirrels on your feeders, you have to outmaneuver them. You can attach a water heater lid to the bottom of your feeder as a squirrel guard, or place a 24-inch (60 cm) section of 6-inch-diameter (15 cm) aluminum duct pipe, or even stovepipe, over the top of your post and fasten it to the bottom of the feeder. Both methods are discussed on pages 36-38.

One way or another, you can outmaneuver them. It may take several tries. A minister I know, Dr. George Kress, puts it this way: "Man needed something to keep him humble, so

BERRY'S WORLD

GET OUT OF THERE!

THAT SEED IS FOR **BIRDS** — NOT SQUIRRELS

HOW COME IT'S OKAY FOR BIRDS TO EAT HERE, BUT NOT ME?

BIRDS HAVE DIFFICULTY FINDING FOOD IN THE WINTERTIME.

WELL, SO DO I.

BIRDS SING!

WHAT DO YOU WANT TO HEAR? HOW ABOUT A LITTLE "MOON RIVER"? ...

Reprinted by permission. © 1980 NEA, Inc.

God made the squirrel.'' If you fix some of your feeders so the squirrel can't get to them, you can make a feeder just for squirrels.

Make a wire basket from chicken wire, or use an old birdcage, as I do. Remove the bottom of the cage and fasten the cage upside down to a convenient tree. Place a couple of ears of field corn in the feeder. The squirrels will thoroughly enjoy pulling the kernels off the ear, eating the germ portion, and discarding the rest. The discarded portion is not wasted, for the ground-feeding birds will eat it.

Fox squirrels too enjoy field corn, while flying squirrels would much rather visit your bird feeder for smaller grains. Flying squirrels visit our feeders every night. In order to be certain there will be enough food left for them to eat, I always fill the bird feeders in our backyard in the evening.

Squirrels enjoy having their own feeder—an old bird cage, with the bottom removed, and hung upside down. Field corn is excellent in this feeder.

There is one important point about positioning the feeders that will be used by flying squirrels. Feeders out in the open make the flyers vulnerable to attacks from owls. Feeders should be placed near trees, or close to shrubs or bushes that offer protective cover where the flying squirrel can escape if attacked.

Gray squirrels and flying squirrels enjoy sunflower seeds, walnuts, raw peanuts, peanut butter, grapes, orange sections, wheat, and most fresh fruits. Red squirrels like all of these things and are said to enjoy suet, too.

Gray squirrels eat some of the foods on a few of our feeders, the birds get some, and then as darkness falls the little flying squirrels come sailing in. We watch by the red floodlight as they come in to the feeder. We will frequently find five or six of these tiny gentle squirrels on the feeder at one time. In contrast to the gray and red squirrels, who fight among themselves, flying squirrels get along together quite well.

In fact, they usually will nest together in family groups. In the wild they take over abandoned woodpecker nest holes for their homes. But they will accept and use a nest box that you build for them. Since there is a shortage of nest holes in most areas, this is one of the most important things you can do to help flying squirrels.

You build a nest box for flyers just as you would a bird house. Choose good weather-resistant wood. Make it 6 inches (15 cm) square inside and 12 inches (30 cm) deep. Place the entrance hole near the top and make it just 1 inch (2.5 cm) in diameter. A hole this size allows flying squirrels to go in and out easily, but will keep the gray squirrels out. If the entrance hole is too large, the gray squirrels will frequently chase the gentle flyers out of their house and take it for their own. Fasten the house to the trunk of a good-sized tree.

If you wish to build a house for gray squirrels, make it

larger. Build it as you would a wood duck house, but make the entrance hole just 2.5 inches (6.5 cm) in diameter. For a fox squirrel make the entrance 3.5 inches (8.8 cm) in diameter.

Any squirrel house should be fastened to a large, stout tree at least 10 inches (25 cm) in diameter. Put it at least 12 feet (3½ meters) off the ground. Use aluminum clothesline or braided wire clothsline to fasten the house to the tree trunk. Pass your wire through a piece of old garden hose so it doesn't cut into the tree where it contacts the trunk. Run the wire in the hose over a limb where it joins the trunk, and then carry the ends to the opposite side of the trunk and secure them to the house. That way the limb keeps the wire from sliding down the tree trunk and you don't have to make it so tight that it cuts into the bark. A securely fastened, well-built house will be occupied almost at once.

If your plantings include fruit and nut trees, then you are providing for squirrels as well as birds. Squirrels also enjoy the winged seeds of the maple trees and the seed in the pine cones. They will eat almost any seed-type fruit. This is one reason commercial nut growers do their best to wipe out the squirrel population around their trees.

In one test 420 walnuts were planted on a 2-acre plot. Gray squirrels were allowed to come and go as they wished. In nine days the squirrels had found and dug up 413 of the 420 walnuts. By fourteen days they had found 419. Knowing squirrels, I will bet the only reason they didn't take the last one was because it was rotten.

Some homeowners dislike squirrels because if they can't find nesting spots in the trees, they will sometimes gnaw through screens over house ventilators and move into an attic. The best way to handle the problem is to nail hardware cloth over the inside of all ventilators. Then put a trap in the attic. Use a trap like Hav-a-Hart, which captures the squirrel without hurting it. Bait the trap with peanut butter. Check it regularly. Release the squirrels you catch out of doors. Soon you will have no more unwelcome houseguests.

But not everything about squirrels is bad. They do plant the nut seeds of many trees in the ground. Those they don't find later grow into new trees. They also make a warning, barking noise that alerts birds in the area when a predator is about. A cat can't catch a smart squirrel. They will harass the stray house cat that comes into your sanctuary until the cat becomes discouraged and leaves. They usually see a hawk before the birds do. While they have been guilty of robbing some bird nests on occasion, I am sure they save more birds than they destroy.

Certainly they add something to your yard. They are the most outwardly visible sign that your efforts to create a sanctuary are working. Their nimble acrobatics are fun to watch, and their casual impudence commands respect if not affection.

·12·
Frogs, Toads, and Other Creatures

Having a sanctuary means more than having a spot for blue jays and squirrels. It also means making your outdoor environment attractive to a whole spectrum of creatures. The more diversity you create in habitat, food plants, sheltering spots, and available water, the larger the number of creatures you appeal to. The more creatures you attract, the more nearly balanced will be this ecosystem, or little world, you create.

Creatures such as frogs, toads, lizards, turtles, snakes, butterflies, beetles, mantises, moths, and many other insects all have a part to play.

This idea of having a home for everyone must be balanced with the reality of your space. A pond for turtles, frogs, and wading birds is great, but not very practical for a small backyard. But water in a small wildlife pond of any type is enough to attract dragonflies and certainly can be home for mosquito-eating minnows. If this isn't practical for you, the

Having a sanctuary means attracting insects as well as birds and mammals. Dragonflies are one of the useful creatures we enjoy.

plastic garbage can lid set into the ground filled with water will attract a host of creatures you may not see.

A sheltered hedgerow with berry bushes may induce a wandering tortoise to establish its home in your yard, and the rockpile that is home for the chipmunks also becomes a sanctuary for skinks, fence lizards, snakes, crickets, and a variety of small creatures. Everything you do has significance.

Naturally the indiscriminate use of insecticides will hurt your sanctuary program. The insects are an important part of the community you are building. They break up organic material so it can be used for plant food; they pollinate flowers, trees, and shrubs that will produce the berries and nuts you need. Insects are food for birds, small mammals, and many of the reptiles and amphibians that come to your sanctuary.

Without the insects and the necessary functions they perform, your sanctuary would be about as efficient as an automobile missing a wheel. When you appreciate what they do and how much we need them, you can be more tolerant when they temporarily forage on some of your plants.

We all enjoy seeing butterflies in our yard. Their colorful fluttering from plant to plant is something you can encourage with the wild flowers you plant. Specifically, there is a member of the milkweed family called butterfly weed, *Asclepias tuberosa*. This is a hardy plant that grows in dry sandy soil and along creek banks. All it requires is some sunshine and it will live up to its name. It blooms most of the summer and adds a colorful orange blossom wherever it grows. Seeds can be obtained from many of the suppliers listed in Appendix I.

Butterflies are not only attracted to this plant, but enjoy great varieties of flowers. They will also flock around your watering spot, sucking up moisture with their long tongues.

Spiders are considered to be the most numerous of land invertebrates. Their webs, studded with dewdrops, are the visible beauties that betray their presence. Spiders feed on smaller insects and in turn serve as a primary food source for small wrens, hummingbirds, and many others. In a healthy environment there are several thousand spiders in an acre of meadowland.

Leaving a log to rot in the wooded corner of your sanctuary offers a home to many beetles and other insects that break

Butterflies add color to your yard. This butterfly weed attracts them.

down the wood and turn it into beneficial humus for the soil. Leaves that have been raked from your lawn, and your neighbors', spread thickly under the shrubbery, offer homes to earthworms, grubs, and other creatures that serve as food for

Having toads move into the sanctuary means you are doing a good job. They eat many harmful insects.

robins, thrushes, towhees, and other birds. In the end the leaves too become humus and fertilize the ground where they were spread.

Toads will move in where there are insects. Toads find a moist, dark, sheltered spot under the edge of your shrubbery or under a sheltering edge of a rock for their home. At night they emerge to stand guard along your woodland pathways, devouring insects that fly or scuttle in their direction.

While a toad may leave and make its way to water for mating after a warm spring or early summer rain, it will do its best to return to its home afterward. Toads have been known to live in one spot in a yard for several years. They come to know the people who live there, and some even learn to come out for a tidbit when called. When you see that a toad has come to live in your yard, you can be assured you're doing a good job.

It's hard to tell people not to hurt snakes, because so many people have an unreasoning fear of them. But let them have a home in your sanctuary, too. There are only a few poisonous snakes. The majority of these creatures are useful and beneficial. Garter snakes eat grasshoppers, crickets, and other insects. Larger snakes eat mice and rats. Some of the larger nonpoisonous ones will eat poisonous snakes that are smaller than they are. And then snakes themselves serve as food for owls, hawks, skunks, raccoons, and other wild creatures. They deserve a place in your sanctuary.

We could make a case for offering a home to almost every spider, amphibian, reptile, mammal, or bird, for in the "web of life" the existence of each depends upon another. As you become involved and make your sanctuary a better place for some creatures, it should become better for all.

·13·
The Plan

You and I have basic requirements, such as food and water, if we are to live. Shelter—protection from the elements,—improves the quality of our lives. It is the same for birds and other creatures. There may be differences in specific requirements, but food, water, and shelter are fundamental to all.

We have discussed each of these elements. Now is the time to decide what you need to attract the birds and wildlife of your area to your backyard. You have many choices. It is up to you to select the ideas that appeal most to you and that fit your circumstances.

How you intend to use your space becomes your plan. It need not be involved, or it can be extensive. But it should suit your situation.

As has been said, the more variety you can provide in food and shelter, the more creatures you will attract. This is an established fact. Curt Jansen, a wildlife biologist who studied this point, found that yards with a variety of trees, shrubs, grasses, and other plants attracted between 30 and 180 species of birds and other creatures. They visited, nested, and found shelter in these yards. In yards of grass and a few trees or shrubs, less than 20 species of wildlife visited each year.

A person living in an apartment high above the treetops will have a hard time attracting wild creatures. Birds normally fly from tree to tree and don't go very high except during spring and fall migrations. If you have no yard or patio at all, you may be limited to a waterer, a bird shelter, and a feeder fastened to your windowsill or window box. Even a windowsill sanctuary will attract some birds. Windowsill feeders and examples of shelters are available from many of the catalogue suppliers listed in Appendix I.

Most of our suggestions are for the city or suburban homesite. If your family has a large farm or ranch, consult with the county agent and local soil conservation officer for help. They will give you a great deal of assistance and many suggestions for forming a comprehensive wildlife plan. The single most beneficial thing that a farm or ranch can offer wildlife is space—living space and nesting space. It will also provide food plants. These are the same things you provide on a smaller scale on a suburban yard or lot.

The first step is to evaluate what you have. See what space can be used to better advantage. Identify the plants, shrubs, and flowers now growing on your site. If you can't identify them from books, take branches, leaves, or stems to your science class, library, or local plant nursery and ask for help.

Draw a sketch of the yard with each plant and tree in place. Now consider how each plant is attractive to wildlife. Does it have berries? Does it offer dense foliage for nesting sites or protection from cold winter winds? Ask yourself what you can do with just a little effort to make your place more attractive to wildlife. What other projects, feeders, houses, waterers, and specific additional plantings would suit your yard?

190'

Beech — Oak Mountain ash Oak

60'

Sidewalk House Mowed lawn

Red maple Patio

Pyracantha Dogwood

Honeysuckle

A. olive

140'

Mowed lawn

Pond

Dogwood

Apple Pear Shrubs and low bushes

White pine

106'

LEGEND

To be planted

Existing

Plant privet and holly hedge

120'

Allow to grow up in native grasses and wild flowers.

A sample plan of a lot, yard, or acreage, showing existing trees and structures, and the proposed additions to make it a sanctuary.

One of the easiest and simplest improvements is to select a strip at least four feet wide in your yard and let it go unmowed, so it can grow back wild and weedy. Not only will this save you energy, but the weeds will gradually be replaced by native wild flowers, grasses, and shrubs that will attract a variety of wild creatures. Rabbits, songbirds, katydids, lizards, mice, quail, and many others will move in to call it home.

Creating a sanctuary that will be attractive to wildlife does not mean that you must turn your yard into a jungle. Even a well-manicured lawn can have a place in your plan. Great numbers of spiders, leafhoppers, and a hundred other species of insects live there. Earthworms, snails, and many small animals call it home. Robins, towhees, mourning doves, sparrows, and at least a dozen insect-eating birds find lawns very attractive foraging spots.

But by all means start with a plan. It may be enough to visualize in your mind how you want your yard to look, but it's much better to write your ideas down. We all have a habit of forgetting that good idea we had last month. In the sketch of your yard, where all existing trees and shrubs have been noted, add what you wish to change or plant.

I have the best luck by keeping my plan in a folder stuck between two books in the bookcase. I cut out all the good ideas I see in the newspapers or magazines and place them in this folder. If it's a magazine or book that should not be damaged, I copy the idea on a separate sheet and place it in my folder.

On the top of each sheet I write the category, such as Houses, Plantings, Feeders, Water, Waterers, Wild Flowers, or whatever. Then when I want to improve my general plan, I just select the articles I need to look over and update my sketch.

Your plan can cover a short project, such as putting up a feeder, providing water, and building a few birdhouses. Or it can involve planting shrubbery for food, berries, and nesting sites and even planting nut trees. A plan of this type will extend over many years.

Short-term or long-term, all plans have value. A word of caution: don't overdo. Remember, the trees and shrubs you plant will grow much larger. Be sure to ask when you buy a shrub how large it will be when it is mature. Visualize the space it will take up when it is full grown, and plan to leave open spaces around it to give it room to grow in.

Open spaces are necessary for birds and wild creatures.

They have to have space to feed and forage in, space to fly in, and space to see what creatures are around them that might act as predators. Open spaces are for you, too. You need space to move about through the yard, and space to be able to see and enjoy the wild creatures you attract.

Be sure the plants you choose grow well in your area and soil. Palm trees don't do well in Connecticut, and most apple trees don't make it in southern Florida.

Choose those shrubs and trees that require little maintenance. The most enjoyable shrubs for birds, wild creatures, and people are those that require little pruning, spraying, fertilizing, or other care. Shrubs and trees native to your area are the best in this respect. No matter where you live, there is a variety of plants to try. In desert country you will select different plants and foods from what you would try in Portland, Oregon, but every area has plants that are attractive to wild creatures.

As has been said, if you need information for your area, check with the county agricultural agent, the local Audubon group, or even local nurseries where plants and shrubs are sold. They will let you know which shrubs work best as hedges and which are best planted alone or in a clump.

You have a big start on your plan if there are mature trees growing around your home. Most mature trees produce seeds, nuts, or fruits that benefit mammals and birds. Older trees have insects that attract and furnish food to woodpeckers, nuthatches, and other birds. In addition, old trees generally have holes for nesting woodpeckers, screech owls, flying squirrels, and gray squirrels. If your trees don't, you can provide them with nesting homes in these trees.

Even old dead snags and trees are valuable to wildlife. At least 49 species of birds and 10 species of mammals are dependent upon or find dead trees important as food or places to live. When a tree dies, try to convince the rest of your family that it is still a useful portion of your yard and important to your plan.

If you have a garden, utilize it in your plan, too. Plant extra foods, such as sunflowers, for the wild creatures. After you harvest the vegetables you want, give the birds a chance to harvest what food remains. They will enjoy seeds and the fruits and vegetables you don't need, while rabbits will dispose of the greens. Birds will repay you for what few garden items or fruits they eat by devouring tremendous numbers of insect pests and weed seeds. Till or mulch the garden in late fall for the next year, after the birds and other wild creatures have cleaned up everything usable.

Provide water in your plan summer and winter too if possible. For maximum benefit it should be water that can be used for drinking and for bathing. Particularly in winter, water should be available to the creatures that stay with you during below-freezing temperatures. Ways to keep the water from freezing are discussed in Chapter 6.

Winter in the northern states is the important time for feeding, too. This is the time when energy is needed to produce warmth, and when natural food is most scarce. Your plan must consider which birds might be spending the winter in your yard and the best way to help them. Wild mammals can use help, too.

Shelter, too, is important in winter. Plantings of dense shrubs that slow the cold winds and provide quiet, protected sanctuaries are best. While you are waiting for shrubs or evergreens to grow, there are several things you can do to provide shelter.

Gather up the discarded Christmas trees in your neighborhood. In an out-of-the-way spot make a pile of these trees. This offers excellent sanctuary for songbirds, quail, rabbits, and other creatures.

Provide a spot in the yard where you make a brush pile from branches trimmed off trees and leaves collected from your yard and your neighbors'. You can add to your brush pile each year. It can't get too big, and the branches will gradually rot down. Or, if you have enough space, you can make several. A brush pile offers a great deal of security to many birds and wild creatures. A rock wall or rock pile offers sanctuary to still others.

The pleasure of sharing your yard with wild creatures is a rewarding reason to make up a plan for attracting wildlife.

All of these points go into your plan. Regardless of what specifics you decide on for your plan, don't make work of it. Do it because you enjoy it and because you enjoy sharing your yard with the wild things. Build your birdhouses when you can enjoy the satisfaction of working with wood and have the satisfaction of seeing the finished houses hanging in the trees. Choosing the proper shrub, and planting it, should be enjoyable tasks—both for the pleasure of seeing that your effort lives and the greater enjoyment of seeing wild creatures harvest its fruit.

·14·

What Others Have Done

If you look at the work involved in creating a total sanctuary, you will probably say, "It's too much. There is no way I can do that." But that is not so. It does not have to be done all at once, not this season, this year, or even over ten years. A look at what others have done will serve as an inspiration. And once you start, the hardest part of the job is done.

Robert Vanderpoel, an editor for the *Chicago Sun-Times*, and his wife created a sanctuary in their backyard. Wooded paths wind through the wildlife plantings and lead past a small, beautiful wildlife pool. The yard has become a place where they rest and where he can "recharge his spiritual batteries."

Tom Ellis, a Florida Game Commission researcher, turned his backyard into a tropical wonderland that draws birds and wildlife like a magnet. Tom started with a small wildlife pool, too. He added rocks to landscape his pool and to make a waterfall. A pump lifts the water from the pool to the top of the rock slide. This oxygenates the water, keeping it fresh. A

112

turtle moved in, and frogs have made it home. Tree frogs sing in the foliage around the pool at night. Anoles, the "chameleons" of the Southeastern U.S., slip through the wet grass nearby. Woodpeckers, warblers, and many other birds find the whole yard to their liking.

Ed and Betty Komarek of Thomasville, Georgia, turned the grounds around their plantation home into a world-famous wildlife sanctuary. One entire wall of their dining room is a plate-glass window that overlooks their wildlife pool and several bird feeders. All types of birds and wild creatures visit the Komareks' yard. Ed and Betty have shared their view of the sanctuary with hundreds of visiting schoolchildren who come to their home on field trips. Scientists and ornithologists record and photograph rare migrating birds from the window in spring and fall. Betty's enthusiasm has stimulated many of her visitors to create sanctuaries of their own.

In Indiana, Wayne Bessinger has taken on a much larger project. He is turning an entire farm of eighty acres into a sanctuary. A portion of the marshy area became a large pond where Canada geese now nest. Each year more young geese are raised. They don't compete for food or space with the wood ducks hatched in the houses that line the banks. The shoulders of the lanes leading through the sanctuary have been planted with autumn olive. This produces a berry that is an excellent fall and winter wildlife food. Not just a few plants, but 10,000 of them are scattered over the farm-refuge. Pheasants, quail, and many other birds reap the benefits of this man's work.

He does all the work. But because of the size of the project, he gets considerable planning help from the Conservation Service and the Indiana Game Department. They provide some plants and even pay a portion of some development costs. That way a comprehensive sanctuary to benefit the largest numbers of wild creatures will be realized.

Others have found other ways to help. Rachel Carson, the author of *Silent Spring*, had a backyard sanctuary. Her love of wild creatures and her scientific training led her to write her famous book, focusing attention on insecticide abuses and dangers. When she brought these concerns to public attention, the public demanded that something be done. The result has been the elimination of many harmful insecticides and thousands of changes in control, supervision, and how these substances must be used. Not only have millions of wild creatures benefited, but we have, too.

I mentioned earlier Dr. Zeleny's work with bluebirds. His own project of building houses, giving talks, and setting up trails stirred great numbers of people to get involved. In a recent report 76 people in Maryland and Virginia told Dr. Zeleny that they had put out and were caring for 1,688 nesting boxes that fledged almost 4,000 baby birds.

You don't have to write a book, as Rachel Carson did, or landscape your entire backyard, or remodel your house to benefit wildlife. Just start! Make a feeder, make a birdhouse, or plant a nut-bearing tree. Remember that old saying: "How do you eat an elephant?" The answer is: "One bite at a time."

Sometimes the understanding and enthusiasm of just one person can change the world and make it a little better for all of us.

·15·

Get Involved

You must be interested and concerned about wild
creatures, or you wouldn't be reading this book.
And I am sure you are saying to yourself, "I'd like to do these
things, but can we afford it?" I can't answer directly, but I
wonder if those of us who care about wild creatures can afford
not to do something.

Each year millions of acres of woodland and farmland are
covered with concrete and asphalt. Fencerows on farms are
being removed, weedy patches of brushy cover are being
eliminated with herbicides, and intensive farming is using land
that once belonged to wild creatures.

Porpoises are still being killed on the Pacific coast, and
whales face the same fate that our bison faced a century or so
ago. On islands in the Gulf of St. Lawrence the eggs of murres
and other seabirds are still being gathered illegally. Baby
guillemots are captured and turned into "pigeon soup." Puf-
fins returning to their nests are caught in nets, and their young
are left to starve.

I could go on and on, but the point is that with all these

things working against wild creatures, we have to join with those who feel that the earth belongs to wildlife, too, and help them. The bison have come back because someone cared; pronghorn antelope recovered from their low ebb of 25,000 to over 175,000 because someone cared. Deer and turkey have rebounded because people were willing to work and speak out for them.

In terms of dollars, it can be very expensive to have professionals landscape your yard for wildlife. But you need not do that. You can plant a few bushes, trees, and plants in your yard each year. Buy small plants. These are less expensive. And in just a few years you will have fruit- or nut-bearing plants. The effort spent mowing a section of lawn can be used to prepare housing for wild creatures and spread leaves under shrubs.

Plan your plantings so they generally improve the appearance of your yard. For it has been established time and time again that each dollar spent for improving your yard makes the whole place more valuable. Cared-for plantings are like putting money in a savings account. Plants for wildlife are an investment that earns money over the years.

But that is not what you and your family will remember. No, it will be the first time a new birdhouse is used, the antics of young rabbits on the lawn, the calling of quail at daybreak, and a cluster of baby quail learning to scratch for seeds under your feeder.

I have never met a person who started caring for wildlife in a yard who didn't find it personally rewarding. To many it has become the highlight of their lives. It's a hobby that offers more than just the satisfaction of viewing various birds and wild creatures. Even with your eyes closed or as you do other things around the house, you will hear singing, twittering, and calling. At night, the song of the owls adds interest and beauty to the night. A flicker may pound on the downspout of your

To me, the reward lies in winning the trust and confidence of a creature.

house in the springtime. But this is a temporary annoyance and a small price to pay for the whole season the flicker family will spend working for you, hunting ants, grubs, and other insects from your yard.

If you decide to join those who think it's important to help wildlife, plant a pyracantha bush this year. In some areas it's called "firethorn." At least 17 different birds find it a favorite food. Bluebirds, pileated woodpeckers, mockingbirds, cat-birds, thrashers, and waxwings are some of them. They and the others will find their way to your plantings. Then put up at least one birdhouse. Take time to evaluate your yard. Ask yourself, "How does our yard help the wild creatures sur-vive?" You are important and what you do is important.

Rachel Carson, just before she died, wrote, "We live in a time of challenge, which is also a time of opportunity."

Appendix I

Selected Lists

A. Excellent groups you may wish to join:

National Wildlife Federation
1412 16th St. NW
Washington, D.C. 20036

Annual Membership $9.50
includes beautiful monthly
magazine

North American
  Bluebird Society
P.O. Box 6295
Silver Springs, MD 20906

Student Membership $7.50
includes quarterly publication

B. Books you may wish to purchase
  (available through your local bookstore or at the addresses listed):

*Audubon Society Guides
  to North American Birds*
Alfred A. Knopf, Inc.
Random House, Inc.
400 Hahn Road
Westminster, MD 21157
There is one for the eastern
  region and one for the
  western region.
$9.95 each

*Harper & Row's Complete Field
Guide to North American Wildlife*
Eastern Edition by Henry H. Collins
Western Edition by J. Ellis Ransom
Harper & Row, Publishers
Keystone Industrial Park
Scranton, PA 18512
$17.50 hardcover
$12.95 paperback

119

Birds of North America:
A Guide to Field
   Identification
by Chandler, Robbins, et al
Golden Press
Western Publishing Co.
Department M
1220 Mound Avenue
Racine, WI 53404
$7.95 hardcover
$4.95 paperback

The Bluebird, How You Can
   Help Its Fight for Survival
by Lawrence Zeleny
North American Bluebird Society
P.O. Box 6295
Silver Springs, MD 20906
$5.50

Field Guide to Eastern Birds
Field Guide to Western Birds
Roger Tory Peterson
Houghton Mifflin Co.
2 Park Street
Boston, MA 02107
$9.95 each

Nest Boxes for Wood Ducks
Wildlife Leaflet 510, May 1976
U.S. Fish and Wildlife Service
U.S. Department of the Interior
Washington, DC 20241
Free

C. Catalogues for Wild Flower Seeds

Gardens of the Blue Ridge
P.O. Box 10
Pineola, NC 28662
(Plants only)
Brochure free

George W. Park Seed Co.
P.O. Box 31
Greenwood, SC 29647
Brochure free

Lofts Pedigreed Seed, Inc.
Chimney Rock Road
P.O. Box 146
Bround Brook, NJ 08805
Brochure free

Vick's Wildgardens, Inc.
Conshohocken State Road, Box 115
Gladwyne, PA 19035
Brochure 25¢

Prairie Nursery
Rt. 1, Box 116
Westfield, WI 53964
Brochure free

Prairie Restoration, Inc.
P.O. Box 327
Princeton, MN 55371
Primarily prairie restoration
Inquiries accepted

Windrift Prairie Shop & Nursery
R.D. 2
Oregon, IL 61061
Brochure 30¢

Conley's Garden Center
Boothbay Harbor, ME 04538
Brochure 50¢

Herbst Bros. Seedmans
1000 North Main Street
Brewster, NY 10905
Brochure free

Soil Conservation Society of America
7515 N.E. Ankeny Road
Ankeny, IA 50021
Seed source list $2.00

Prairie Associates
6328 Piping Rock Road
Madison WI 53711
Brochure free

Prairie Ridge Nursery
Rural Route 2, 9738 Overland
Mt. Horeb, WI 53572
Brochure free

Prairie Seed Sources
Little Valley Farms
Rt. 1, Box 287
Richland Center, WI 53581
Brochure 25¢

Clyde Robin Seed Co. Inc.
P.O. Box 2855
Castro Valley, CA 94546
Brochure free

Plants of the Southwest
Dept. OG. 1570 Pacheco St.
Santa Fe, NM 87501
Brochure free

D. Catalogues for Plants and Shrubs   Free

Burpee Seed Co.
Warminster, PA 18991

Waynesboro Nurseries
Waynesboro, VA 22980

Kelly Bros. Nurseries
Dansville, NY 14437

Stark Bros. Nurseries
Louisiana, MO 63353

Vernon Barnes & Son Nursery
Box 250
McMinnville, TN 37110

Geo. W. Park Seed Co.
P.O. Box 31
Greenwood, SC 29647

Henry Field Seed and Nursery Co.
Shenandoah, IA 51602

E. Catalogues for Bird Feeding Supplies, Feeders, and Houses

Duncraft Wild Bird Specialists
25 South Main Street
Penacook, NH 03303
   (Houses, feeders, supplies)

North American Bluebird Society
Box 6295
Silver Springs, MD 20906
   (Books, birdhouses)

Wildlife Woodcrafters
12601 Buckingham Dr.
Bowie, MD 20715
   (Houses, feeders)

The Bird Tree
5 Swallow Lane
North Oaks
St. Paul, MN 55110
   (Houses, feeders, supplies)

Burd Products
Box 2645
Grand Junction, CO 81501
   (Houses, feeders, supplies)

Beverly Specialties Co.
Box 9
Riverside, IL 60546
   *(Sprays, plastic tubing,
   faucet connections for tubing)*

Hyde Bird Feeder Co.
56 Felton Street
Waltham, MA 02154
   (Birdhouses, feeders, supplies)

Appendix II

Planting a Tree or Shrub

There are two ways to come by trees and shrubs. You can purchase them, or you can find and transplant your own. Purchased shrubs come in a pot or can with soil around their roots, as "bare-root" saplings, or they may be sold with the roots surrounded with soil and wrapped in burlap.

You can plant potted shrubs and trees and those wrapped in burlap any time of the year as long as you do it carefully and remember to water them well weekly until fall. Obviously, any week you have an inch or more of rain you needn't water. If you plant in the fall, they need not be watered as often. In the north there are periods of time during the winter when the ground is not frozen and planting is possible, but it's best to wait until spring.

Bare-root trees are sold in their dormant season and must be planted at that time. This is the time the trees have lost their leaves and are in a resting state. Trees shipped to you will come with the roots wrapped in some moist material, such as moss, wood shavings, or even wet newspapers, which will be covered with plastic or other impervious material to hold the

Left: Open the package and immerse the roots.

Right: Allow the roots to spread out without crowding or folding back on themselves.

water in. Open the package and immerse the roots completely in a container of water for four to twelve hours.

Dig a hole deep and wide enough to allow all the roots to spread out without crowding or folding back on themselves.

Allow the garden hose to trickle into the hole all during planting to be certain that the soil is saturated with water.

Place the tree or shrub in the hole, making sure it is upright. Gradually replace the soil, putting the richest topsoil in the bottom of the hole, in closest contact with the roots. Then, with your fingers, crumble the soil into small bits and gently work it around the rootlets. Use plenty of water, as all pockets of air must be eliminated from around the roots if your tree is to be healthy.

Fill the hole with loose dirt until it is up to the same level it was when the tree was growing in the nursery soil.

Mound the soil up to create a cup-shaped depression around the tree. The depression around the trunk, with a dam of soil around the edge, will hold the water till it can soak into the soil when you water your tree. Do not fertilize your tree the first year after planting.

If you dig and transplant native trees or shrubs from the woods or from a neighbor's property, there are a few points to remember. It is easiest to identify a tree or shrub when it has leaves or fruit, but this is the most difficult time to transplant. The time to transplant is when the trees have shed their leaves and are dormant. Mark the plant you intend to transplant with a piece of string or plastic ribbon while it has its leaves, so you can find it later in the year when it has lost its leaves and is dormant. The dormant period is usually from November to March in the northeastern and western states, but may only be the month of December or January in the deep south.

If the tree is 6 feet (2 meters) high or taller, it is a good idea to use your shovel to cut some of the roots during the growing season, several months before transplanting. Draw a circle around the tree 18 inches (45 cm) from the trunk. Sink the shovel straight down into the soil to its full depth, then pull the shovel out. Repeat this all around the circle. This cuts all roots within 8–10 inches (20–25 cm) of the surface, and stimulates the tree to put out the many short rootlets that will help keep it alive when you transplant.

If your tree is small—less than 24 inches (60 cm) tall—you can usually transplant it even during the growing season.

When removing the tree, dig up a large ball of earth with the roots and handle the plant carefully and gently to be sure that the soil stays around the roots until it is secure in its new home.

A shrub or tree in a pot or pail, as you get it from the nursery, is planted similarly. Before putting the tree in, dig your hole as deep as the pot and soak it thoroughly. Soak the plant while it is still in the pot. Turn the pot upside down and gently slide out the plant and the soil in one piece. Place it in the hole carefully, to assure that it will be planted at the same level in the ground that it was in the pot. Gently place new soil around the pot soil and firm it into place.

The key to successfully transplanting any plant or tree is faithful watering. Place your hose where it can gently trickle at the base of the plant thirty minutes every day the first week after transplanting, then twice weekly for two weeks, then weekly until fall.

Planting trees and shrubs is easy; you can do it successfully.

Appendix III
Building a Bird Feeder

To build a roofed tabletop feeder you need the following materials:

1. A piece of exterior plywood 24 inches (60 cm) square and ½ inch (1.25 cm) thick. (Exterior plywood is made with glue that holds even when the wood becomes wet.) A similar piece may be used for the roof. One or both pieces can be obtained where lumber is sold.
2. Four pieces of wood 8 inches (20 cm) long for corner posts. Any size will do, but pieces about 2 inches (5 cm) in diameter look most attractive.
3. A water heater top 20–24 inches (50–60 cm) in diameter, for a squirrel guard, to be placed on the feeder pole.
4. A dozen wood screws 1–1⅛ inches (2.5–2.8 cm) long and 4 shorter screws to fasten the squirrel guard to the feeder. A few small nails or wood screws for the roof, and one lag bolt 3–4 inches (7–10 cm) long to fasten your feeder to the post. Lag bolts can be obtained at any hardware store. While you're there, buy a large washer. This will be used to help hold the feeder more securely.

5. Two pieces of wood 24 inches (60 cm) long that rest on the tops of the corner posts and support the length of the roof.

6. A piece of metal or rigid plastic for the roof. Must be at least as big as the base. Metal or plastic is better for roof than plywood.

7. Four slender pieces of wood about 24 inches (60 cm) long for railings to keep the seeds from blowing or falling off the platform. Wood material called "quarter-round" in ½-inch (1.25 cm) size can be purchased at lumber or hardware stores. It is inexpensive, soft to work, and will make your feeder look professional.

8. A post 4 inches (10 cm) in diameter and 6 feet (2 meters) long.

Make sure your plywood piece is square, for it makes it much easier to cut the railings, roof, and other pieces. With sides of equal length, one measurement is all that is needed to cut four railings and your roof material.

Cut all four corner support posts to the same length. Fasten each post to a corner of your plywood base by standing the post up on a level work surface, placing a corner of the base on the post, and drilling a hole through base and post. Choose a drill bit slightly smaller than the diameter of the screw, and drill only to a depth slightly less than the length of your screw.

Place a screw through both holes and tighten it with a screwdriver. Repeat at all corners and turn feeder right side up.

If your roof is to be plastic or metal, attach short boards across the tops of the posts to help hold the plastic up and to keep it from sagging. Regardless of roof material selected, roof supports add strength to your feeder. Attach roof supports to corner posts with nails or screws.

If you are putting a squirrel guard on the feeder, now is the time to attach it. Turn the feeder upside down. With the guard in position, drill four holes around the perimeter of the guard and fasten it to the base with short screws.

Also drill a hole in the center through both base and guard, where your lag bolt fastens the feeder to the post. Choose a drill bit *slightly* larger than the lag bolt, so the bolt fits through easily. Try to put the hole in the middle of the feeder for balance.

Drill a hole in the top of the post that is slightly smaller in diameter than the lag bolt and almost as deep as the bolt protrudes from the feeder.

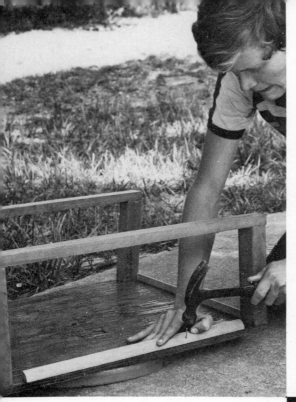

Turn your feeder back right side up, measure the distance between the posts, and cut your quarter-round railing material to fit. Make your railings short enough to allow for a gap at each end, so any water that blows in can run off. With small short nails that won't come through the base, nail the railings to the feeder base.

Now put on your roof. A plastic sheet can be fastened to the supports with short screws or short nails. A plywood roof can be screwed to the support posts. For the top, use a piece that is slightly larger than the base (this overhang will protect your feeder from blowing rain) and attach with nails or short screws. Select the spot in your yard where you want your feeder to be, and dig a hole. Place the post in the ground so the top is level with your chin (to allow you to see into the feeder for cleaning and filling), then pack the dirt tightly around the base of the post.

You will need some help placing your feeder on the post. Put the large washer on the bolt. Place the bolt through the feeder and into the hole. While your helper keeps the feeder balanced and steady, tighten the lag bolt with a wrench. If you are planning to paint your feeder, do so after it has been mounted. An unpainted feeder will weather well, but it will last much longer if it has paint protecting it from repeated wettings. Avoid lead-based paint, for flaking paint chips can be poisonous. Use light-green or -brown matte-finish paint.

When the paint is thoroughly dry, place a pint or so of wild-bird grain in the center of the platform. In the course of a day, most of the birds passing through will have found it. If they haven't, put some food on the roof to attract their attention. Clean your feeder each time you refill. A gentle brush with your hand will knock off seed hulls and trash, so you can add new food. If the squirrels in your yard are smart enough to get over your squirrel guard, add the predator guard described in Chapter 7 or the stovepipe guard mentioned in Chapter 5.

Appendix IV

Building a Birdhouse

A. *Material required for a Bluebird House*
   One board 6 inches (15 cm) wide and 6 feet (2 meters) long
   and ¾ inch (1.87 cm) thick—or the equivalent
   in smaller pieces.
   Set of small hinges and screws
   Several dozen 6-penny box nails
   Hook and eye for latch
   Aluminum scrap 7 × 9 inches (16.8 × 21.6 cm) for roof
   cover

B. *Tools required*
   Hammer
   Saw
   Screwdriver
   Drill with ¼-inch (.6 cm) bit
   Square
   Wood rasp or file
   Tin snips

134

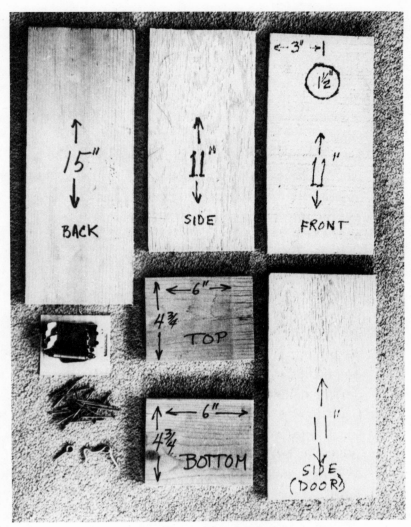

Parts of the bluebird house, including hinges, nails, hook and eye

C. Directions for construction

Houses for all types of birds are built in a similar fashion. Choose the lumber to fit the dimensions of the house you wish to build. Your final *bluebird house* should have a floor approximately 6 × 4½ inches (15 × 11.4 cm), and the interior should be at least 8 inches (20 cm) high. The entrance hole should be exactly 1½ inches (3.8 cm) in diameter.

1. Measure and cut three pieces 11 inches (28 cm) long from the board. These pieces will be the front and two sides.
2. Cut another piece 15 inches (38 cm) long for the back panel. The extra length allows you to nail or fasten your house to a pole or fence post.
3. The bottom piece, or floor, should be cut 6 × 4½ inches (15 × 11.4 cm). Saw a little bit off each corner to make drainage and ventilation holes.
4. You can make the top the same size as the bottom, or larger to overlap the sides and front piece.
5. Drill the entrance hole 1½ inches (3.8 cm) in diameter in the front panel. Place the entrance hole so it is centered from side to side and so the finished hole rises 6–8 inches (15–20 cm) above the floor. If your drill doesn't have a bit large enough to make a hole that size, draw a circle that size on the board, and drill small holes around this circle, connecting the holes. When this has been done, you will have your opening. Or drill a smaller hole and saw to the right size with a saber saw or a jigsaw. File or sand the entrance hole smooth.
6. Hold or tape all pieces together before you start nailing to be certain they fit, and so you can see how each must be nailed to the other. Then nail together all parts except for one side.
7. Fasten the remaining side to the back panel using hinges and small wood screws. Use a hook and eye to secure and lock the side door. I prefer the side hinged

Bluebird house partially assembled. Side door is to be fitted with hinges and hook and eye.

door to a front opening or a removable top because a side door seems to snag less on the overhanging roof when you open it. Also, it gives easy access to the interior, making it easier to clean.

8. After the door is in place, nail a piece of soft metal to the top of the house for a waterproof roof. It should be an inch (2.5 cm) larger than the house all around, to give good overhang for rain protection. I use scraps of

Pass wire around the trunk and fasten it to itself. The plastic hose protects the tree trunk from damage.

aluminum. I fasten my roof up and over the protruding back panel, so it folds down behind the house. This protects the open grain of the wood back panel and, as mentioned, gives forward slope for rain runoff.

Equally important, it creates an air space between your metal roof and the wood top piece that makes the house much cooler in summer.

9. Drill a couple of holes in the protruding upper and lower back panel, and nail or run wire through the holes to fasten the house to a pole, fence post, or tree.

10. The house can be painted or left to weather naturally, as you prefer. If you decide to paint, don't paint the inside, and be sure to paint several months before the spring nesting season to give the house time to air out.

Appendix V

Christmas Tree for Wildlife

Why not make a Christmas tree for the birds and other wildlife this year? It could be a project for a family or a class.

The tree need not be an evergreen; any tree can be used. The important thing is that it be low to the ground, so you can reach it on all sides. For you will hang garlands of food from the boughs as you would put tinsel on your tree at home. The ornaments for the tree will be food for wildlife, too.

Make garlands, or strings, of foods the birds like. Some of the best things to use are popcorn, raw peanuts, cranberries, green peas, raisins, cubes of cheese, bits of apple, and any other fruit you have. Use a heavy long needle, such as a rug or upholstery needle, and kite string or nylon line to string the foods you select into long ropes. A garland can be mixed to make a multicolored strand as you alternate popcorn and cranberries, or you can make a garland of one food.

When attaching the hard bits like cranberries or peanuts, go through an edge of the cranberry or peanut rather than through the middle. That way the bird or squirrel doesn't tear up your garland tugging at the food, but pulls it loose easily. Drape the finished garlands on the tree.

A wide variety of foods can be used as ornaments. You can fasten sugar or butter cookies with holes in the center to the boughs with string. Pack the rough surfaces of pine cones with peanut butter and hang them about the tree. Ears of field corn add color and are an excellent food for your tree. Apples, chunks of pumpkin, and pieces of suet can be threaded on string and used as ornaments. Suet cupcakes (see pp. 29–30) can be placed on the boughs and tied in place.

Use your imagination and what you have available to add to these suggestions. And, if you have time, send me a picture of your Christmas tree for wildlife.

William J. Weber, D.V.M.
Rt. 1, Box 368A
Leesburg, FL 32748

Index

143

About the Author

William J. Weber, D.V.M., is a veterinarian with 25 years of experience in private practice in Leesburg, Florida. The Weber family home is in the midst of a lakeshore wildlife sanctuary. Dr. Weber's writing and photographs appear regularly in wildlife and nature magazines. He is the author of *Wild Orphan Babies: Caring for Them, Setting Them Free*; *Wild Orphan Friends*; and *Care of Uncommon Pets*.